THE HISTORY OF IDEAS IN SOCIAL WORK

Haluk Soydan

In association with the
Social Work Research Association

VENTURE PRESS

Published by
VENTURE PRESS
16 Kent Street
Birmingham
B5 6RD

British Library Cataloguing-in-Publication Data
A catalogue record for this book is available from the British Library

ISBN 1 86178 022 2   (paperback)

Cover design by:
Western Arts
194 Goswell Road
London
EC1V 7DT

Printed in Great Britain

This book was translated by Roy Fox

Contents

LIST OF TABLES AND FIGURES **Page**

Preface to the English Edition

Since first being published in 1993, this book has been extensively used within Swedish, and to some extent in other Scandinavian, social work education and training programmes. It has also been presented and discussed at international seminars and workshops, especially thanks to a revised and abridged version of one of the chapters which was published in the Scandinavian Journal of Social Welfare. Encouraged by the interest of colleagues, students and social workers who read the book or the journal article, I felt it was time to introduce the book in English in order to reach a larger group of students of social work.

I perceive this book as a modest contribution to the social work discourse that aims to define the identity of social work as a discipline and as a professional practice, and to strengthen its legitimacy. I hope that the opportunity of reaching a larger group of readers will stimulate others to contribute to this discourse, which today very much needs to be carried forward. I am grateful to professor Malcolm Payne of the Manchester Metropolitan University and the other members of the advisory committee of the Social Work Research Association Monograph series for promoting the book for the benefit of the social work community.

Haluk Soydan
Stockholm, September 1997

Preface

Social work has been established in Sweden as an academic and research discipline since 1977. This change has naturally brought to the fore the need to state the core of the subject and to define its boundaries, especially in relation to neighbouring sciences such as sociology, psychology, and social policy, among others. Swedish social work has no self-evident tradition to lean back on, despite the fact that it is now formally an academic and research discipline.

Attempts are made to contribute to an understanding of the core and boundaries of the subject. These attempts are either limited to the question 'What does the subject do?', that is, a description of questions that researchers in the discipline occupy themselves with, or to the question 'What does the world around look like?', that is, an indication that a particular factual area belongs to one's own discipline.

'What has the discipline achieved?' is my point of departure. This means that I work from a history of ideas approach. Several disciplines have investigated their traditions through a history of their ideas as a step in their seeking for the core and boundaries of their subject. Studies in history of ideas are highly-identity-developing through the way in which they illuminate trends in ideas and because of the fact that they are self-reflecting. The purpose of this book is to throw light on social work through a history of its ideas.

Studies of the history of ideas in social work have been studies of social work as a practical activity. Studies of the history of ideas in social work as a scientific discipline are rare or in a proper sense lacking. The task of this study is therefore to argue for the illumination of social work through the history of its ideas as a scientific discipline. Because of the state of research, my work is directed towards the development of concepts and exemplification. The door will thus be opened to a scientific dialogue in which my conceptual contributions, with all their merits and shortcomings, are a contribution to this dialogue. From that perspective, I see my work as investigative.

I am convinced, and this conviction is based on the experience gained in other sciences, that an important factor in the struggle of social work for scientific recognition is to establish its roots in the development of social science.

This would clarify many questions that advocates and students of the discipline have asked themselves.

The various parts of this work have been the subject of discussions and viewpoints at many seminars and lectures, both in Sweden and abroad. I would like to thank those colleagues and students who have given their views on my work on those occasions. Some of my colleagues have taken great pains to read parts of the manuscript and have given invaluable opinions: these are Gunnar Bernler, University of Göteborg; Sten Höglund, University of Umeå; Lisbeth Johnsson, University of Göteborg; Monica Johansson and Rolf Stål, University of Örebro; Jorma Sipilä, University of Tammerfors; and Pablo Suarez, University of Uppsala. Björn Eriksson of the University of Uppsala has also been a great source of inspiration through his book *Samhällsvetenskapens uppkomst (The origins of social science)*. Many thanks for your invaluable ideas and support! The writer alone is of course responsible for any omissions in this work. I would finally like to thank the Faculty of Social Science at the University of Uppsala for putting their research resources at my disposal.

Örebro 1993

Haluk Soydan

Chapter 1
The Inquiry – Delimitations and Method

Most people perceive social work as a profession in which one works with people. Social work as a profession is oriented towards social problems. For many people, the social worker is a professional person who takes care of deprived, needy, and weak people in society.

In the minds of the public it is natural to relate certain occupations, or professions, to distinct sciences. The medical profession is an established profession which in the public mind is associated with 'medical science', even if the profession is nowadays served by a number of specialised sciences such as histology, physiology, bio-chemistry and so on. People also know that the science of upbringing and education is called pedagogy. But it is more doubtful whether the same question can be put about the police profession. Is there such a thing as a police science? Or are there other sciences that contribute with their knowledge to the police profession? It is, for example, criminology, sociology, pedagogy, and law that produce knowledge necessary to the police profession. It is difficult to associate a single science with the police profession itself. What is the position with regard to social work? Can social work as an occupation be said to have its own scientific basis which the profession is built on? Or is social work a profession that is dependent on several scientific disciplines? Can a profession on the one hand have its own scientific discipline, and on the other use the knowledge bases of other disciplines? What does this mean for the development of the profession and its own discipline?

The subject of this book is social work as a scientific discipline. In this respect, social work is to be perceived in the same way as other social and behavioural sciences. As we shall see later in this book, the idea that social work is a social science, and should be developed as such, is not new. The idea has a history going back more than a hundred years, even if the discipline of social work in itself was institutionalised at a later stage through the integration of the subject into the university structure.

Every social science discipline contends for scientific and intellectual recognition. We can almost speak today of a status hierarchy of sciences. This ranking is more or less pronounced, more or less conspicuous. It most often consists in an unspoken and hidden hierarchy, but can nevertheless be measured with the help of some indicators. We can naturally ask professors and students themselves about what they consider to be the status of their own discipline in relation to other sciences. We can also ask the general public to survey how much prestige the discipline in question enjoys in their eyes. But there are also other indicators that may be used, such as, for example, the resources allocated to the discipline, the productivity of its research, pioneering theoretical and method-ological contributions within the subject, and so on. Between different faculties, but above all between different disciplines within the same faculty, there seem to be 'stronger' and 'weaker', 'better' and 'worse' disciplines. These types of value judgements are naturally also based on extra-scientific factors, but intra-scientific factors such as, for example, the precision of definition of the core and boundaries of the subject, the range and number of theories and their degree of sophistication, methodological insights and instruments, play a decisive role in determining the position of the discipline in the scientific community. The more limited and well-defined the research object of the discipline is, the greater the prestige the science seems to enjoy. The more sophisticated theories a discipline has in its armoury, the greater the power and prestige the discipline seems to have. Within the field that social work belongs to, different degrees of precision for the determination of their core and boundaries are applied in different disci-plines. Some disciplines have more obvious objects of study: national economics studies the economy, political science the State, psychology the human mind. It is less evident for other disciplines. Taking one of the most established social sciences as an example, sociology is a discipline that is con-stantly fighting to determine its core and boundaries. Sociology constitutes a good example of a discipline that has devoted itself to charting the development of the history of ideas in the subject. This has been a way of contributing to the discipline's struggle for scientific and intellectual recognition.

The central task of this book is to present some glimpses from the background of the history of ideas in social work. My starting point is that the discipline must start to investigate and systematise the roots of the history of its ideas. I consider this to be necessary if the discipline known as social work is to have a chance to reach its core and gain a certain amount of clarity as to its bounds. In its turn, this process is identity creating and identity reinforcing – factors that social work needs in its striving towards scientific recognition.

Social work is a practical activity when its aim is to help people with some sort of social problem. In such cases, social work has been organised within the framework of a definite structure and has special working methods to tackle these problems. Social work as a degree course subject has as its aim the insti-tutionalisation of the subject within the framework of a country's higher education structure. This means that the subject has been established as a sci-entific discipline, that a chair in the subject has been created, and that certain types of degrees are awarded in the subject. Social work as a research tradition refers to the discipline as a specific *set of ideas*. I shall return to these aspects of social work in more detail. It is sufficient to state as a start that it is the last aspect of social work that constitutes the central focus of this book. Social work as a research tradition, as a scientific discipline or as a definite set of ideas is a concept that will serve to point the way towards the problem areas covered in this study. It is not easy in a presentation of a history of ideas to keep apart the various lines of development that have influenced social work. To a certain extent these aspects develop hand in hand. Even if it is difficult to keep the various aspects apart, my aim has been to bring out what is relevant for social work as a research tradition and the specific set of ideas that belong to the discipline.

Description types

When social work is studied from historical and history of ideas perspectives, different types of criteria can be selected. This involves deciding upon the application of certain criteria for the demarcation of the presentation of the history of ideas.

History of ideas studies of social work have most often been studies of the *organisational and institutional development* of social work (see, for example, Bruno 1948, Davis 1967, Kahn 1959, Pumphrey 1956, Wald 1938). Since social work has primarily been conceived as a practical activity, that is, a profession the task of which is to help people in need, it has been most convenient to show most interest in the different forms of organisation of this help. The focus of these studies has been mainly on organisational development. Interest in the formation of the ideas, that is which ideas and concepts that lay behind the organisation of the help, the work of social change, which sets of ideas that have lived on in various historical contexts and so on, has come second as a question following on from the presentation of organisational development. Very little explicit interest has been shown in the development of social work as a set of ideas in a scientific context. As the object of this study is social work as a scientific discipline, the organisational development of social work lies outside the scope of the study.

Another type of description emanates from the criterion that man is by nature prepared to help other people (see, for example, Swedner 1983, 1985). *Man's mutual willingness to help* as a criterion of studies in the history of ideas has resulted in attempts to penetrate social history as deeply as possible in order to find the oldest indications of mutual help that can be defined as social work. This has meant, for example, the study of ethnographical finds and literary descriptions of human problem-solving with elements resembling social work.

Another aspect of this type of description is that it has been based on man's striving to *change* society; 'the spirit of human progress', or the Law of Progression as the Scottish scientist Adam Ferguson named it, as a criterion for identifying actions that can be defined as social work. This as a starting point can bear little fruit if we are to study social work as a scientific discipline.

A third description type is to limit oneself explicitly to the scientific develop-ment of the discipline of social work, that is, social work as a *definite set of ideas*. The starting point here is that social work has its own set of ideas and concepts and that this set of ideas is specific for social work. By using the set of ideas specific to social work as a criterion, it is possible to delimit the subject in relation to other subjects. It is this thought that lies behind those definitions of the subject set up by various writers, examples of which are given in the next chapter. In this context, a serious problem is that there are great difficulties in specifying a well-delimited field for social work. The problem is that what is considered to be specific to social work is something that may also be found in other disciplines. However, this situation is not unique to social work. The same goes also, for example, for the neighbouring science of sociology.

> *'There are also very tangible real difficulties in narrowing down the specific sociological field. The problem is that what we call sociologi-cal analysis is not exclusively carried out within the academic discipline of sociology. Such analyses have instead become an integrated part of most of the social sciences. Political science, for example, has drawn its analyses of voting behaviour from sociology. Pedagogical analysis of classroom dynamics is from the same source. Within the historical sciences, sociological analysis has become the most common and largely forced out earlier chronological analysis. The inner cohesion of sociology and its boundaries to other subjects have therefore been more and more eroded'* (Eriksson 1988:26).

The problem for the discipline of social work is that what is defined as social work is also carried out within the framework of other disciplines. If sociology can be regarded as an exporting discipline, social work may be generally con-sidered an importing discipline as far as theories and analytical methods are concerned. The boundaries between social work on the one hand and sociology, psychology and social policy on the other have been fluid. In certain cases there have existed, on the whole, no boundaries at all. In other cases, possible boundaries have not been developed. Regardless of which discipline has had sole rights to, or preferential right of interpretation of, certain areas of knowledge, it has not been possible to develop boundaries to provide social work with a well-delimited conceptual field.

Attempts to establish the bounds of the subject and to state its ideas content may be made in different ways:

a) we can study what social work researchers actually research;

b) we can try to delimit a certain factual area of social life and assign it to the discipline of social work; and

c) we can study what has been achieved within the discipline (Eriksson 1988).

If we choose the first way, we study current research interest among active researchers. We chart the research projects in progress, the scientific issues being studied and the scientific findings and state of the art of the discipline. Such a survey provides knowledge of the current state of thinking, but hardly of history of ideas perspectives.

The second way of stating the boundaries of the subject is to assign studies of a certain factual area of social life to the discipline of social work. Such attempts are constantly being made. One common way is to assign studies of social problems to the discipline of social work. A problem with this type of delimitation is that it is not only social work that works with social problems. Now and then, there arise confrontations between different disciplines which lay claim to a specific area such as 'social problems'. Another problem with this type of subject delimitation is that changes in social reality force various subjects to adapt their concepts, which means, among other things, that the boundaries between different subjects are altered. It is thus an extremely difficult task for a presentation of the history of ideas to identify such socially delimited areas for social work.

As a third way of delimiting the discipline of social work, we can ask the question *'What has the discipline achieved?'* Then we have automatically built in a historical perspective on its conceptual development. We have thereby declared that we are interested in the discipline's *tradition* – the development of its history of ideas. But how, then, is social work as a scientific discipline to be understood and approached?

How a science or sciences are to be described is far from obvious. Such subject areas as history of science, history of ideas, philosophy of science, and sociology of knowledge reveal many aspects that complicate the description of sciences, that is the delimiting of scientific work from other knowledge. There are opinions and scientific traditions that differ from each other on decisive points. Different scientific conceptions emphasise different criteria in different ways. If you were to agree, for example, with the conception of science of

Desmond Bernal (1965), the great historian of science, that social science can only be regarded as a science if it uses the methods of the natural sciences, large parts of social science would have to be declared non-scientific. If modern sociologists were to follow the criteria for scientific knowledge laid down by the philosopher of science Karl Popper (1959,1972), lines of argumentation in many research works would look different, and at the same time many works would be declared unscientific.

It can, on the whole, be maintained that the concept of science has two aspects: on the one hand it involves the systematic presentation of knowledge, and on the other the systematic accumulation of knowledge.

> *'Science, then, is the working rules and judgement norms, the method,which are to be used to guarantee and improve the contents of the knowledge that we gather about the world. The sciences are the knowledge that has been accepted, or which at one time was accepted, as being valid, and, not least, which has logical and genetic connections with knowledge put forward later. This means that the concept of science contains two power centres, two starting points for activities of very different kinds.*
> *One of them is oriented towards the presentation of new knowledge, the other towards the systematisation of already established knowledge. The scientific method, "the systematics", thus constitutes one type of knowledge development, while the scientific knowledge, "the history", constitutes another'* (Eriksson 1988:30).

When seen from the viewpoint of its history of ideas, social work is perceived as one of several sciences. The same as other sciences, social work is expected to have a history of collected knowledge, methods and positions achieved. Those sciences that have taken great pains to chart their history have a better overview of their development and sets of ideas. Unfortunately, social work does not have this kind of overview.

In spite of a lack of systematic studies of what the discipline has achieved, it can be claimed that there is a kind of attitude towards our social surroundings which may be presumed to constitute a sort of core of social work. It is a basic scientific undertaking to hold together three elements: to have a theory of society or of man as a social being, to have a programme, a scheme for changing problematic situation, and to have a group of people committed to carrying this change through. These three elements can hold together in different ways. The development of their history of ideas may take different forms, and different factors can be emphasised to varying degrees in different forms. But irrespective of what the development of its history of ideas and trends is like, we have a basic way of looking at social work as a scientific discipline. The overall aim of this book is to present some glimpses from such a history of ideas context. I wish to show concepts and sets of ideas that characterise social work as a research tradition. I see the core of social work in its striving to integrate theory, programmes of change, and agents of action. In addition, it constitutes an exciting challenge as regards philosophy of science. There are some trends in the development of its history of ideas which coincide with areas claimed by other disciplines. This should not constitute an obstacle to studies of the development of the history of ideas in social work. Those areas to which several sciences lay claim will certainly remain in the indefinite future.

Inventory of problems

As hinted at in the introductory discussion, we are moving here in a problem area that lacks recognised research tradition. How is social work as a scientific discipline or research tradition to establish roots in the development of the social sciences? What type of conceptual instrument can be used in such investigations? What is the accumulated knowledge of the development of the history of ideas in social work? Questions of this type should be the object of systematic investigations. The answers are of crucial importance for the development of social work as a scientific discipline.

Starting point. A first step in the present work is to develop a conceptual frame of reference. The purpose of this is to provide a structure to history of ideas studies of social work as a scientific discipline. As working instruments, theoretical frames of reference are indispensable. They provide a structure for an extensive and far-reaching empirical field. They thus make it possible to handle a large amount of empirical material which is, for the moment, unsorted. In this sense they fulfil the same function as Max Weber's (1949) 'ideal types'. The conceptual frame of reference structures a context by peeling away details and bringing out what is typical of social phenomena. This creates opportunities for the production of scientific knowledge. But it can also be claimed that every conceptual frame of reference means limitations, and these consist mainly in the exclusion of alternative interpretations. With this insight in mind, I perceive the theoretical frame of reference of the study as being provisional. New knowledge and new insights will, naturally, lead to a revision, or even a rejection, of the conceptual instrument. These are the conditions of working on a provisional basis. They are also the conditions of science.

The conceptual frame of reference of the study is also to be seen as hypothesis generating in so far as it sorts an empirical material and motivates new angles of approach to the material studied. In Chapter 2, there is a general discussion of social work as a concept and of the necessity of rooting social work as a scientific discipline in the tradition to which the social sciences belong. In this chapter, I also present the theoretical frame of reference that forms the basis of this book.

Special studies. This book is not a catalogue in which thinkers and practitioners who in one way or another are connected to social work are presented. Neither does it claim to present all the so-called classics which can be considered important to social work as a set of ideas and as a specific scientific field. The working method that I choose, and which I also consider the most reasonable, given the conditions of the task in hand, means that, with the help of the conceptual frame of reference, I select those thinkers, practitioners or history of ideas traditions necessary to exemplify and illustrate central lines of development in the history of ideas within social work.

In Chapter 3, I investigate Saint-Simon's and Saint-Simonism's social philosophy and concept of science as a basis of the historical roots of social work. The fact that this history of ideas tradition, for the first time in the history of the social sciences, formulates a basic attitude specific to social work makes Saint-Simon's thinking particularly important in this context. The basic attitude comprises three separate but connected elements: a *theory* of society and of man as a social being, *a programme* of how social problems can be handled, and a *group of people* who carry out the work of social change. In this chapter is also discussed a continuity of ideas from Saint-Simon to the welfare work carried on in Sweden in the 1930s and 1940s, and to the commissions of inquiry whose work in the 1970s formed the basis of the 1982 Social Services Act. This task occupies a relatively large space in the book, and my motivation for this is that Saint-Simon has so far been unrecognised in studies of the history of ideas in social work.

In Chapter 4, I present Mary Richmond as a central practitioner and thinker, and as the first person to formulate the scientific frameworks for work of social change oriented towards the individual. Her efforts also constitute an example of a development trend which may be considered specific to social work; that social work as a set of ideas has its *genesis* in practical experience.

In Chapter 5, I follow some interesting lines of development in the history of ideas which link the Richmond tradition within social work with the attempts of psychology (as well as its claims) to develop Richmond's work oriented towards the individual. Both before and after the breakthrough of the Richmond concepts of 'social diagnosis' and 'social casework', social work has been influenced by psychology. I give a short description of these influences in this chapter. This is traditionally the field of knowledge of psychology, a field that social work touches on as the discipline develops independent theories.

In Chapter 6, the work of Jane Addams is presented as a foundation of the development of the history of ideas in social work. Jane Addams serves as an illustration of a central line of development developed in opposition to the tradition created by Richmond. The Addams tradition has ideas connected to the tradition discussed in chapter 3 in connection with Saint-Simon.

Finally, in Chapter 7, the book brings together some of the threads from the other chapters. By following up some of the lines of reasoning from the first two chapters, I attempt to show a connection between a definition of the discipline seen from the history of its ideas and a definition of the field of knowledge of the discipline as it is elaborated in Swedish research today.

Chapter 2
Theoretical Framework

Introduction

Ever since social work was established as an academic discipline with its own academic chairs, there has been a growing need to establish a base for the discipline in the context of its history of ideas. This base is necessary if a discipline is to get a clear idea of its theoretical and methodological roots and of its role in society. Many people have posed the question of what exactly social work is. Both stipulatory and programmatic definitions have been given, but no agreement has been reached as to the core, boundaries, objects of study, theories and methodology of the discipline.

I perceive social work as practice and as a scientific discipline. This point of departure is not problem free, but is perhaps the only one possible. We still lack a reasonably-well-worked-out frame of reference for studies and assessment of ideas in the history of social work. Are there any traditions of thought and action in which we can find the roots of social work? Who are the originators of these traditions? In other words, are there any so-called classics in which we can find the roots of social work as a discipline and as practice. What right does social work have to lay claim to certain classics? Are there any criteria by which we can claim that social work can be rooted in traditions of thought and action, as well as in the classics? In such a case, what are the traditions of thought and action in social work? What kind of delimitation problems are involved in relation to other disciplines? In this chapter, I aim to develop a theoretical frame of reference for studies and assessment of social work from the perspective of a history of ideas.

A possible starting point for studies of this kind is man's need of help and the innate propensity of human beings to give help. When choosing this point of departure, the focus will mainly be on social work as *practice*. The scientific dimension will be left aside. Another starting point is to seek the historical roots of social work in traditions of thought and action where social work as practice is grounded in scientific thinking and scientific activity. It is the latter that is the point of departure of this chapter. The practice of social work to help people in need of help and to change people's condition of life for the better are connected to scientific analysis in a given historical context. From the viewpoint of a history of ideas, this is dependent on two developments: the emergence of scientific analysis of society during the eighteenth century and the application of scientific social analysis and of prognosis as instruments for the work of social change.

To show how social work as practice can be grounded in a social science tradition, I have used Björn Eriksson's study (1988) of the origins of social science. In his account of the origins of scientific social analysis, I find the scientific roots and scientific basis of social work. In those thinkers who were the source of scientific social analysis, I also find the idea of 'the spirit of human progress', which is of importance to social work as practice and as scientific activity. It is against this background and in my analysis of social work that it can be claimed that social work consists in three components: practical activity, an academic discipline, and a research tradition. A study of traditions of thought and action that analyse society, and that carry forward the work of change based on the spirit of human progress and on an innate propensity to give help, reveals two tendencies that can be refined from the history of ideas. I call these tendencies in the evolution of the history of ideas 'from theory to practice' and 'from practice to theory'.

The work of social change aims at changing what is regarded as undesirable or as a social problem. A central issue in traditions of thought and action is whether it is people or society that constitute the basis of social problems. In other words, the question that is traditionally asked if we look at the history of ideas is whether it is people or society that is sick.

Since social work has its roots in the evolution of the social sciences, the question of its relationship to other disciplines and activities arises. In this chapter, I shall discuss its relationship to the discipline of sociology. These two subjects have at least two points of intersection. The first is their interest in studies of social problems, and the second is their interest in social change and the work of social change.

My presentation leads to a theoretical frame of reference developed by means of a cross-tabulation of the variables *the interaction between theory and practice in the history of ideas, and the nature of the causes of social problems*. With my frame of reference, it is possible to: (1) classify classical thinkers and practitioners so as to be able to see differences and similarities between them, and study the history of ideas leading up to modern thinking in social work; (2) justify why the classics studied can be regarded as being the classics of social work.

Homo ad juvendum paratus as a starting point
Professor Harald Swedner, the holder of the first chair of social work in Sweden, has devoted special attention to issues concerning the history of ideas tradition in social work. Knowledge of, and insights into, the historical roots of the ideas of a scientific discipline are necessary both for extra-scientific reasons, mainly for satisfying the need for legitimacy, and for intra-scientific reasons, mainly those

concerned with theory and methodology. Swedner (1983) has primarily chosen an inductive approach in his work. His point of departure is *Homo ad juvendum paratus*, that is, the person who is prepared to help others. He has attempted to construct a 'tree of ideas', a kind of typology in which a number of thinkers and practitioners are classified. Swedner starts out from two established concepts in the philosophy of science and theories of knowledge, namely idealism and empiricism. The theorists and practitioners mentioned are classified in accordance with these concepts. There is no discussion of how they are related to each other or of how they are assumed to constitute a logical or empirical whole.

Swedner (1983:160) also uses other concepts.

> *'I set out from a continuum ranging from "revolt" to "reform".*
> *Naturally, in this work, I have not been able to avoid having the left-right dimension in mind, but still I have tried to look upon the problem of classification in an unbiased way, and, as best I could, I have attempted to take into account the whole spectrum of problems and controversies that you come across in the history of intervention thinking. This left-right dimension is reflected, among other ways, in the division of work of change into that which is **directed from the grass roots** and that which is **directed by the authorities**, as implied in the base of the tree of ideas'*
> *(emphasis original).*

Swedner thus uses several dimensions: idealism and empiricism, revolt and reform, and that of Left/Right (in the sense that the concept is used in political analysis). The typology results not only in the division of 'grass-roots-directed' and 'authority-directed' work of change, but also in 'actor thinking' and 'spectator thinking', used by Swedner to denote two polarised attitudes towards social work.

Swedner differentiates between eight forms of 'actor thinking', that is different traditions in social work, which developed during the 1960s and 1970s. He calls these traditions: political action, community education, community work, action research, philanthropic social work, evaluation work, community development, and, finally, reform work. As regards traditions that are in harmony with 'spectator thinking', he mentions in his tree of ideas hermeneutics and critical analysis, and logical empiricism and linguistic analysis. The tree of ideas includes 64 thinkers/practitioners, but the number mentioned could have been considerably larger and Swedner (1983) admits that 'I have not yet been able to place many interesting "spokesmen" in my schema'. Here he mentions people such as Lenin, Wittgenstein, Parsons, Habermas, Sartre, and Feyerabend, all of whose work spans a wide spectrum of theoretical thinking.

Furthermore, Swedner points out that in his schema he has not made any attempt to include 'ways of thinking' and 'spokesmen' that have been mainly concerned with the work of change at the individual, family, and small-group levels (such as psychoanalysis, sociodramatic therapy, group-dynamic therapy, family therapy, casework and network therapy). This statement is, of course, only partially correct since Mary Richmond, for example, to whom Swedner devotes special attention, is a person who is considered to be a good representative of social work at the individual and small-group levels.

The earliest thinker included on the tree of ideas in social work is Copernicus (born 1473), but the unfinished lines reaching back into history suggest that the tree can be extended even further.

In a later work, Swedner (1985:10-11) writes:

'As early as in the oldest well-documented societies – the Sumerian Empire in the Iraq of today, the Egypt of the Pharaohs, ancient China, ancient Greece and the Roman Empire – there is a division of labour that points towards the development of professions specialising in care and social welfare, principally doctors and midwives, but also people responsible for the material well-being of the population.'

In an even later work, Swedner (1987), basing his ideas on a book by the Finnish writer Mika Waltaris, *Sinuhe, the Egyptian*, has tried to trace the roots of social work further back in history. The book refers to conditions in Egypt in the fourteenth century BC over a period of 30-40 years. Sinuhe, who comes from the lower classes, is educated as a scribe and eventually becomes a doctor at the royal court in the capital, Thebes. Sinuhe also leads an eventful life as one of the Pharaoh's supply depot administrators and devotes himself to helping the poor in Thebes. He is eventually banished to an outlying district of the nation on account of differences of opinion with the Pharaoh. There he leads the life of a hermit, watched over by guards. Muti, a woman he got to know earlier in his life, comes to visit him. It is in the relationship between them, claims Swedner, that we meet the first 'home help'. This home help is described in the book as a wise woman who supports and exhorts her ward, and creates the conditions for a meaningful life for Sinuhe during his last years. Swedner also states that Mika Waltari describes things that show the development of welfare professions; that of the doctor, of the supply depot administrator and of the home help. Swedner's point is that our conception of social work as being a recent phenomenon, which we mainly associate with the education of trained social workers in Sweden and some other countries, is a very misleading one.

We find a similar way of reasoning in the French-Croatian researcher Yves-Rastimir Nedeljkovic. He also seeks the roots of social work in human sociality and in being compelled to help each other. In his opinion, being interested in one another is the world's oldest occupation. It is a matter of spontaneous activity.In a lecture on the historical background to social work as science and as practice, he said (1989):

> '*It is the heritage of human mutual relations, based upon elementary mutual help, customs and morale, originating from the necessity to keep alive, all the way to institutions and professions that have been formed and still are being formed by states and governing systems. And they, turned into proverbial and other (today neglected or "forgotten") paradigms of wisdom and skill to form various social bases, according to time and place of human living, have been settling for thousands of years, while the contemporary profession of social workers is hardly aware of the depth of true roots of its own activity.*'

The following are the main elements of the historical roots of ideas in social work as seen by Swedner:

- His schema or typology attempts to combine several concepts: idealism and empiricism, revolt and reform, the Left-Right scale, grass-roots-directed and authority-directed social work.

- Swedner's schema is based on an unstated assumption that social help is founded on human sociality and mutuality when it comes to helping each other. This basic assumption is clearly expressed by Nedeljkovic.

- Because of this basic assumption, anybody may, in principle, be included in the schema. This is especially true of thinkers with

  documented approaches to social change, or of people who have themselves been documented.

- Idealism and empiricism seem to be two important characteristics used to characterise the thinkers included in the schema. As presented there, idealism and empiricism are regarded as two poles of one and the same dimension. These concepts are not defined. Above all, there is no discussion of the connection and tension between these concepts, which means that the tree of ideas loses some of its precision. This may be explained, among other ways, by stating that empiricism is a concept from the philosophy of science, while idealism belongs to the battery of concepts used at the ontological level.

- The concepts of revolt and reform, the Left-Right scale, grass-roots-directed and authority-directed social work refer to normative conditions.

An important consequence of the line of argument on which Swedner's tree of ideas is based is that the roots of social work will extend more and more as historians, archaeologists, ethnologists and other scientists widen our historical perspectives and show that, as far back as we know, man has been *Homo ad juvendum paratus*. There is here a further complication into which we do not need to go too deeply, but which should nevertheless be mentioned, and it is that historical and archaeological research shows that man has not only been a helping being but also destructive and self-destructive. The way of systematising the historical roots of ideas in social work presented above provides a perspective on the tendency of human beings to give mutual help: people's sociality. But it does not give us much guidance on understanding the history of ideas background to social work as *practice and scientific discipline*. My point of departure is that the description and analysis of the background of the history of ideas in social work as practice and as a scientific discipline must be rooted in the analysis of the origins of social science.

The origins of social science as a starting point
In this section I shall refer to the Uppsala sociologist Björn Eriksson's study *Samhällsvetenskapens uppkomst. En tolkning ur den sociologiska traditionens perspektiv* (1988). In the perspective that will be presented, the historical background to ideas in social work as practice and as a scientific discipline is to be sought in the breakthrough of social analysis in the eighteenth century, and,above all, in the endeavours made during the nineteenth century to use scientific analysis and prognosis to improve people's condition of life and to remedy social problems.

Eriksson's work focuses on sociology and the scientific analysis of society. In one sense, these concepts go hand in hand or, in other words, the rise of the sociological analysis of society coincides with its social scientific analysis. The modern disciplines of the social sciences spring out of the sociological analysis of society. This sociological analysis thus forms the basis of social scientific understanding of the dynamics of society, including its driving forces, the interaction between its various components, problem-generating mechanisms, and so on. As such, sociological analysis exceeds its own limits and produces concepts and instruments for disciplines that gradually develop out of the process of specialisation in the social sciences. One of the disciplines that slowly develops is social work. Putting social studies on a scientific basis during the eighteenth century constitutes both a foundation and a prerequisite for the development of social work as practice and as a scientific discipline.

But a more concrete and important connection to the scientific analysis of society emerges through the phenomenon that Eriksson calls 'sociology as agent activity'.

During their historical evolution, people have attempted to understand and explain both society and man as a social being from different perspectives. In the course of history, irrational and rational models have been contrasted and replaced each other. Irrational and rational models for understanding and explaining social phenomena, against which sociological (or social scientific) analysis argued, sought the causes of mechanisms for what happens in society outside society. Within the framework of irrational models, it was God or some other being outside society that constituted the basis of explanation. In the thinking of the Greeks and Romans, reason was the guiding principle by which human thought by its own force could understand the meaning and innate order of things. The Greeks, as Georg Henrik von Wright (1986) puts it, were over-rationalistic in their belief in the ability of thought alone, without any foundation in experience, to uncover the truth in the order of things.

After a long period of medieval irrationality, 'belief in reason' was won back in the European tradition. For Descartes, Spinoza and Leibniz, for example, reason was 'eternal truths'. For the philosophers of the Age of Enlightenment, reason was an 'intellectual force' that guided the search for truth. These philosophers were conscious of two tendencies: rationalism and the empirical philosophy of the seventeenth-century philosophers. The philosophers of the Age of Enlightenment during the eighteenth century thought that they had combined the best elements of these two tendencies. John Locke developed his ideas on empiricism: for Locke, a human being was at birth a *tabula rasa*, a blank page, and a passive recipient of impressions from outside. All knowledge had its origin in impressions coming from outside. David Hume, who had considerable influence on the growing Scottish school of philosophers, claimed, on the other hand, that people were independent and active seekers of knowledge.

The central thesis pursued by Eriksson (1988) is that the sociological analysis of society 'originated in all its fundamentals during the Age of Enlightenment'. The 'sociological analysis of society' is a much wider concept than that implied by the word 'sociology'. Here we think of concepts and working methods in sociology and neighbouring disciplines such as, for example, economics, political science, psychology, and social work. This argument is reinforced by a number of more exact definitions. Firstly, Eriksson refers to the emergence of the *continuous* sociological tradition. The existence of isolated approaches now and then in history does not cause the displacement of the starting point. Secondly, Eriksson's presentation refers to 'the actual origin of this tradition, not in any sense its nominal origin'. Thirdly, the decisive point of transition is located in 'the late Age of Enlightenment and within the group of social philosophers and historians that are usually called the Scottish School'. It is a common belief (see, for example, Aron 1968, Zeitlin 1981) that the emergence of social analysis is ascribed to the Enlightenment, and that the French Enlightenment philosophers are given a central role in this process of change. The originality of Eriksson's contribution lies in the fact that he demonstrates that the scientific or sociological analysis of society underwent a revolutionary transformation through the work of the Scottish School, with Adam Smith, Adam Ferguson and John Millard as the central figures. Their work is based on the so-called four-stage theory, whose principal features can be summarised in four points. First, society is a system in which the various components of society are dependent on each other. These different components are linked by horizontal relationships whose interconnected changes constitute what we call history. Second, the dynamics of society are independent of the intentions of single individuals. The activities of single individuals form the basis of societal development. Third, society has grown at the cost of the individual. This relationship between the individual and society has meant that the individual has become more and more civilised and is more legally secure, but individuals have also become more dependent on society and imprinted with societal factors. Fourth, despite the fact that societal development is unplanned, with no goal or end, society shows a large number of patterns that can be discovered by the scientist.

In summary, we can establish that the Scottish School laid the foundations of modern social science. They carried out an analysis of history and explained the mechanism of change in society. Consequently, they laid the foundations of the work of social change that is based on scientific analysis. But they did not make any predictions about future changes in society. The scientific analysis of society was to wait for some time more before its theories of society were linked to the work of social change. The history of ideas in the nineteenth century was rooted in the eighteenth-century scientific analysis of society, and developed the central theme that sick social conditions should be changed by means of scientific models and theories. In this sense, developments during the nineteenth century are of central importance to social work.

The spirit of human progress
If we assume that the aim of social work as practice is to solve social problems, a question that will be discussed later, Ferguson's 'Law of Progression' is of particular interest. The Law of Progression was one of three basic assumptions

concerning human nature that we can find in the work of the Scottish thinkers. The idea of the spirit of human progress is naturally much older than the Scottish school. Ferguson was of the opinion that human beings strive continually to improve their conditions of life. He wrote that people were not created to rest, and that they were constantly making improvements and continually learning from their mistakes.

It is in the nature of human beings to endeavour to develop society for the better. From this basic assumption it is not far to the idea that social work has its roots in human sociality and mutual need of help. The Scottish writers call this 'the bettering of circumstances', that is a progression from less good to better conditions. This parallelism is also reinforced by the Scottish writers' second basic assumption about mankind, called 'sympathy' by Smith, which deals with a phenomenon that in modern social work is covered by the terms empathy and perspective. The assumption is fundamental to all social work. Smith wrote:

> '*As we have no immediate experience of what other men feel, we can form no idea of the manner in which they are affected, but by conceiving what we ourselves should feel in the like situation. . . By the imagination we place ourselves in his situation, we conceive ourselves enduring all the same torments, we enter as it were into his body and become in some measure him, and hence form some idea of his sensations, and feel something which though weaker in degree, is not altogether unlike them*'
> (quoted by Eriksson 1988:313).

At the end of the eighteenth and beginning of the nineteenth centuries, widespread social upheavals were taking place. The French Revolution affected the whole European political scene, and the need for social change was great. Analysing changes in society up to the present and not attending to future changes in society, as the Scottish writers did, was alien to how thinking about social scientific progress developed in the nineteenth century. If you had analysed changes in history, you could, and indeed must, make predictions about the future in order to build a society that worked better. You had to construct a philosophy of history that would form a moral foundation for social change. How else could you do anything about the political chaos that prevailed in society? The sick society had to be cured. This changed attitude towards the overall role of social science in society was a central element in nineteenth-century thinking. Eriksson considers Marquis Marie Jean de Condorcet, although he died in 1794, to be a predominant figure in the nineteenth-century history of ideas and its striving towards a better society free of social problems. Condorcet worked on the basis of scientific analysis and knowledge. He wrote his *Esquisse d'un tableau historique des progrés de l'esprit humain* in 1793, and it was published posthumously in 1795. In it, Condorcet gave a description of how mankind has developed. His presentation finished with a future vision of human society. Condorcet calls this phase 'progrés futurs de l'esprit humain', the future development of the human spirit. For Condorcet, human progress was inevitable, as it was based on mankind's capacity for achieving perfection, called by Eriksson 'perfectibility'. According to Condorcet, mankind had a built-in driving force that knew no bounds and which guided human society forward to a better condition.

> *'The idea of human perfectibility is similar to the thought of the desire for change, the law of progression, but is more demanding and, to a certain extent, has more consequences. The desire for change is aimed at man's external conditions. People constantly attempt to alter the conditions of their lives so that they can function a little more simply, a little more efficiently, produce considerably better results for slightly greater effort etc. . . The thought of perfectibility is also aimed at the inner consequences of external work; people will be ethically and existentially better, so to speak, and more perfect from this work'* (Eriksson 1988:384).

Condorcet hoped that the state of things in the future would mean the best possible perfection. In his presentation of the phases of development in the history of mankind, he also emphasises the decisive role of science and knowledge. The road to perfection was scientific knowledge. According to Eriksson, however, Condorcet did not seriously consider the scientific connection between the present situation and the final stage he had in mind. Condorcet 'went direct to the final situation and tried to outline its characteristics. In so doing, he set the tendency that was to prevail during the nineteenth century: theories of history were combined with philosophies of a condition of society which was different'. The philosophy of history thus states *what can be done* to achieve a better condition of society.

The theory of history of the Scottish writers and the philosophies of history that developed in the nineteenth century in Condorcet's footsteps complemented one another. The idea was that the problem-generating social conditions, the sick society as they said at that time, could be changed for the better by using a theory of history or a scientific analysis of society, which in its turn was linked to this philosophy of history. This was the central theme of the nineteenth-century tradition in the history of ideas. Many writers could be mentioned within the social sciences. Henri Saint-Simon, August Comte and Karl Marx, just to name a few, were central figures in this development. They and other figures in the history of ideas are regarded as central classics of, above all, sociology. In this connection, Eriksson discusses the concept of 'sociology as agent activity'. My thesis is that this development in the history of ideas can also be ascribed to social work, and I shall return to this notion in a later section.

What is social work?

This question is more and more often raised by both practitioners and researchers in social work. Here I shall distinguish between three independent but interrelated concepts to explore what social work can involve. It is important analytically to keep apart social work as *practical activity, an academic discipline* and *a research tradition*. Hans Berglind, a professor of social work in Sweden, has implied a similar distinction. He uses the terms 'academic discipline' and 'research field'. Hans Berglind does not, however, develop this distinction but concentrates on a discussion of the 'research field' of social work, with attention focused on the concept of 'social problem'.

In the literature, it is usual to distinguish between social work as practical activity and as an academic discipline and/or research tradition (see, for example, *Vad är socialt arbete?* 1981, Berglind 1983). Instead of 'academic discipline', the terms 'research field', 'research discipline', 'academic subject' and so on are also used. In the literature, social work as an 'academic discipline' usually denotes both the discipline and the research tradition.

Another way of approaching the question of 'what is social work?' is to distinguish between social work as practical knowledge, social work as theoretical knowledge with a practical orientation, and social work as theoretical knowledge. Here attempts are made to answer the question by pinpointing different types of knowledge that characterise the different elements that make up social work. Differentiating forms of knowledge in this way also corresponds to the dual concepts of social work as practical activity and as an academic discipline, where the latter is equivalent to various types of 'theoretical knowledge'. In the next section, I shall discuss these three components, which, in my opinion, constitute social work.

Social work as a practical activity

Social work as practical activity aims at helping people who suffer from some kind of social problems. By 'social problem' I mean, in accordance with

Rubington and Weinberg (1971:6), 'an alleged situation which is incompatible with the values of a significant number of people who agree that action is necessary to alter the situation'. This is a limited way of characterising social work as practical activity since it does not include any indication of preventive social work at the individual and group levels, or of community work. But the traditional literature on social work is very rich in this type of definition. The earliest and most distinct definitions are to be found in Mary Richmond's works, and refer to social work as casework. As examples, here are some definitions from her works and those of others:

> '*The art of doing different things for and with different people by cooperating with them to achieve at one and the same time their own and society's betterment*' (Richmond 1915:43).

> '*The art of bringing about better adjustments in the social relationships of individual men, or women, or children*' (Richmond 1917:389).

> '*Those processes which develop personality through adjustments consciously effected, individual by individual, between men and their social environment*' (Richmond 1922:98).

> '*A method of helping people out of trouble*' (de Schweinitz 1924:ix).

> '*A particular way of assisting people to meet their personal and social needs*' (Lowry 1937:264).

> '*A process through which we use the understanding of the individual in society in the rendering of certain social services supported by the community and applied for by members of it*' (Gartland 1940:126).

> '*A therapeutic discipline for encouraging ego-development*' (Wilsnack 1946:303).

> '*An art in which knowledge of the science of human relationships and skill in relationship are used to mobilize capacities in the individual and resources in the community appropriate for better adjustment between the client and all or any part of his environment*' (Bowers 1949:317).

> '*Social work seeks to enhance the social functioning of individuals, singly and in groups, by activities focused upon their social relationships which constitute the interaction between man and his environment. These activities can be grouped into three functions: restoration of impaired capacity, provision of individual and social resources, and prevention of dysfunction*' (Boehm 1958:18).

'Casework has always been a psychological treatment method. It recognizes both internal psychological and external social causes of dysfunctioning and endeavors to enable the individual to meet his needs more fully and to function more adequately in his social relationships' (Hollis 1964:1).

'By provision of certain services and material resources and by psychologically therapeutic supports and counsel, casework modifies either the problem experienced in the individual case or the person's modes of coping with it or both. The aim of casework is to restore or reinforce or refashion the social functioning of individuals and their families who are having trouble with person-to-person or person-to-circumstance encounters' (Perlman 1965:607).

In later definitions, there is a shift of focus in social work. Social work began to be understood as two-way communication between social worker and client, which means that the earlier view of the client as an object weakens or disappears. There is increased emphasis on the interaction between the individual and their social environment. The definition presented by Gitterman and Germain (1976:602) is considered representative of the prevailing view:

'Social workers focus on problems in living which fall into three areas: (1) problems and needs associated with tasks involved in life transitions; (2) problems and needs associated with tasks in using and influencing elements of the environment; and, (3) problems and needs associated with interpersonal obstacles which impede the work of a family or a group as it deals with transitional and/or environmental tasks.'

The authors develop this definition in a later book, *The Life Model of Social Work Practice* (1980). Similar lines of thought are to be found in *Inledning till socialvårdsmetodik* (1969) by Marja Almqvist, one of the Swedish pioneers.

Another Swedish writer, Alf Ronnby (1983:13), expresses ideas that go in the same direction: '. . . by social work I mean a set of methods and their professional use to regulate and handle problems when people are not capable of fulfilling their social roles according to prevailing norms and expectations'.

The term *psychosocial work* came into use in Sweden in the 1980s. Bernler and Johnsson (1988) describe psychosocial work as a part of social work and define the concept by stating a number of criteria:

- the interplay between people and their environment is fundamental to personal identity and to the generation of psychosocial problems

- psychosocial work is based on a coherent theoretical perspective

- psychosocial work comprises a set of working methods to be used in relation to individuals, families and other groups for preventive and treatment purposes

- psychosocial work is carried on according to three approaches in which the person administering the treatment influences the client either by their own actions or by direct or indirect control.

Psychosocial work adopts its own profile as its own field of activity, especially in relation to psychology and psychiatry (see chapter 5). The definitions presented here refer to social work at the individual, family, and group levels. A strong tradition prevails when we talk of social work as practical activity. In recent years, two other types of social work have come to the fore, namely social administration and planning; and community work and community development.

Social work as an academic discipline
Björn Eriksson (1988) argues that a discussion of the origins of the discipline of sociology must begin by distinguishing sociology as an academic discipline from sociology as a tradition of social analysis. I am of the opinion that the same analytical standard must be applied to social work. Social work as a tradition of social analysis will be discussed in the next section. Let us here consider the question of social work as an academic discipline.

Social work as an academic discipline is dependent on decisions about educational policies. It often has to do with formal delimitations which do not always correspond to the conceptual boundaries between different academic disciplines. The most recent definition of the discipline of social work was when a chair was established at the University of Lund, and ran as follows:

> '*The professorship in social work is oriented towards research and teaching regarding the causes and methods of solving and preventing social problems at different levels of society. Research within the field of the professorship should be organised in such a way that the results can be implemented in practical social work.*'

The chair in Stockholm is described in a similar way, but with the difference that they emphasise the practical application of the post in more detail. The description runs as follows:

'The professorship in social work is oriented towards the study of social problems and measures for solving them. Included herein is the analysis of both the causes of social problems that affect persons, groups, communities and so on in our society, and the background to the problems in the interplay between the individuals and their social environment. Moreover, the research area includes the analysis of different ways of solving social problems, the development of knowledge that can be implemented in preventive action and the designing of measures that can be applied in practical activities in the social field.

'The needs of education in social work and the experience gained by those who are active in social work are to influence the orientation of research into social work. Research within the field of the professorship is to be organised with a view to implementing research results in practical applications.'

When the post was reviewed in 1990 because of the appointment of a new professor, they kept the same description but left out the last paragraph.

Social work as an academic discipline was introduced relatively late in Sweden. Social work became a teaching subject in social studies in Sweden in 1977, and the first chair in the discipline was established at the University of Göteborg. Further chairs in social work were later created at other Swedish universities. The development of an academic discipline depends on a country's historical circumstances. The rise of a discipline can be connected to intra-scientific and/or extra-scientific factors. Intra-scientific factors have to do with a discipline's internal, that is theoretical and methodical, development where the rise of theories and methods breaks through the boundaries of existing disciplines, out of which new disciplines grow and are established. In this way, academic disciplines and research traditions are linked together. Extra-scientific factors are circumstances that externally force the emergence of an academic discipline.

The conditions lying behind the development of the discipline of social work in Sweden have been described and analysed by a number of authors (Swedner 1987, Brante 1987, Eliasson 1987). The extra-scientific factors proved to be of the utmost importance to the development of social work as an academic discipline. In a study of social work, Thomas Brante (1987:37-38) writes:

'The material reasons for the institutionalisation of the discipline will not be touched upon here. Let me just mention that they naturally have to do with the expansion of the social sector. From 1960/61 to 1964/65, 1,028 persons graduated in social studies, and from 1975/76 to 1979/80, this figure was 8,480. In 1960, one per cent of the country's workforce was

*employed in the social sector, in 1980 this figure was eight per cent. At
the same time, social workers have enjoyed relatively low status and had
low salaries, and this has been an important motive in demands for professionalisation. 'Professionalisation can take place in many different
ways. One possibility is to extend the length of the course of studies and
to supplement this with salary increases. Another, considerably cheaper,
status-raising strategy is to establish research institutions, that is, to
produce scientists who can develop and communicate "esoteric"
knowledge. The expansion of the underlying practical activities,
together with social workers' demands for professionalisation, thus constitute an important condition and reason for research in the discipline
being institutionalised.'*

In summary, it can be stated that it was hardly intra-scientific factors that led to
the emergence of social work as an academic discipline. It was through extra-
scientific factors that social work became institutionalised as an academic
discipline in Sweden.

Social work as a research tradition

If we only go on the basis of the descriptions of the discipline as set out for the
professorships in social work, we shall not get much out of investigating social
work as a research tradition. We shall then be forced to examine 'what is to be
studied' instead of 'what is in fact studied' and 'what has been studied'.
Thomas Brante (1987) comments on the description of the discipline for the
professorship in social work at the University of Stockholm:

*'The description strongly emphasises the importance of practical appli-
cation at the same time as it leaves the field free for interpretations of the
actual content of the discipline. What is the object of knowledge? What
methods are to be used? How does the discipline differ from sociology,
for example? How does it differ from political practice? And, perhaps
above all, what is social work?'*

Brante raises central questions about social work as a research tradition. These
are, and will remain as far as we can see into the future, the most central issues
of the problem areas of the discipline as far as its theories of science and
knowledge are concerned. Because the issues are so central, but, for natural
reasons, as yet unanswered, it is not surprising that the four professors of social
work studied by Brante should all have different opinions on the subject of
research tradition and research discipline. Delimitation in relation to other disciplines – principally sociology and psychology, but also, for example, social
policy and social law – is a particularly difficult problem.

It is my thesis that a more *productive way of approaching these central issues is, from the perspective of a history of ideas, to investigate thinkers, practitioners, movements and traditions in ideas which social work as a research tradition can lay claim to.* We can then ask, for example, the following questions: is Max Weber a classic of sociology or of political science? Is Adam Smith a classic of sociology or of economics? Or are they both? The same type of questions can be posed about social work. Which are the classics of social work? Does social work have its own classics? Can social work lay claim to classics traditionally attributed to other disciplines? Are Saint-Simon and Karl Marx, for example, classics of sociology or of social work?

From theory to practice – research for change

In social work as a research tradition, we can see two main development tendencies in the history of ideas. My terms for these are from *theory to practice* and from *practice to theory*. By the 'from theory to practice' tendency I mean that research results and theoretical knowledge are intended as a foundation for social practice, whether the research is based on current professional and socio-political priorities or merely on issues raised theoretically (intra-scientifically). By the 'from practice to theory' tendency I mean that it is social practice that is the primary consideration, and that theoretical knowledge and research findings are of secondary importance. In nineteenth-century currents of ideas of significance to the development of social work, these two tendencies exist side by side, and to a certain extent are interwoven with each other. This is so because the traditions that develop as practice, and which then attempt to form a theoretical foundation for themselves, are influenced by the theories of other traditions. How these tendencies are interwoven and how this manifests itself in the perspective of developments in the history of ideas are empirical questions that remain to be studied.

The work of social change seen from the viewpoint of the 'from theory to practice' tendency in the history of ideas can be studied in its narrower or wider meaning. The former refers to research explicitly aimed at the work of social change. We can call this 'research for change'. The latter refers to social analysis and social theory used by a group of agents of change in order to change society. In this connection, it should be emphasised that 'social work' and 'the work of social change' are used as synonyms, since all social work, both research and practical activity, aim at social change.

In his book *Historic Themes and Landmarks in Social Welfare Research* (1977), Sidney E Zimbalist studies the type of research I here call research for change. Zimbalist has made a survey of research projects in social work and social welfare carried out in the USA during the period 1870 to the mid-1960s.

The 1870s are chosen as the starting point since organised social work starts to develop with the founding of the National Conference of Charities and Corrections in 1879. References are also given in the book to research work undertaken in the 1970s. However, Zimbalist sets the limit generally as the mid- 1960s, as he concentrates on long-term research themes and milestones whose delimitation is dependent on a longer historical perspective.

Zimbalist (1977:7) uses the concept of 'historical research theme', and writes:

*'In the course of the investigation of the development of research in this field, it was found that there have been a number of distinct "waves" or "cycles" of emphasis in research interest and activity over the years. While they overlap each other considerably and in some instances have either been recurrent or continuous through many decades, nevertheless they tend to be more or less self-contained, coherent, and cumulative trends over a given period. In most cases they may be said to reflect current research "fashions" in the field – swings of the scientific pendulum, as it were – that arose out of current **professional and social priorities**, crystallized and proliferated to a peak of popularity, and then often subsided or stabilized'* (emphasis added).

Starting from this definition, Zimbalist identifies six research themes:

- Research into the causes of poverty
- Measuring the distribution of poverty
- The social survey movement
- Quantification and indexing in social work
- Evaluation research into the effectiveness of the social services
- Studies of multi-problem families.

Other important research themes, such as, for instance, research on welfare administration, research on theories of social work, research on child welfare, are not included in this list since Zimbalist considers that these themes lack continuity and a coherent approach.

An important issue raised by Zimbalist is the delimitation of research in the work of social change. Here he uses both 'social work research' and 'social welfare research' as starting points, as well as research in neighbouring fields, such as, for example, sociological research, psychological research and economic research. Zimbalist (1977) uses the following criteria to identify research in the work of social change:

'1.   Research on a problem or question arising in the practice of – or in the planning of – any of the usually recognized social welfare services or social work programs of the period.

2.   Research conducted by a professional social worker (or the contemporary equivalent thereof).

3.   Research conducted under the auspices of a social work agency, including schools of social work.

4.   Research financed by social work agencies or funding bodies.

5.   Research published in social work journals or through other channels dealing primarily with social work.'

All of these criteria are extra-scientific. Criteria 2-5 refer to the organisational or personnel-related relationship of the research to social work. The first criterion is also extra-scientific, but has in addition to do with the work of social change as such. Zimbalist points out that this research has its origin in current professional and sociopolitical priorities. In other words, the inspiration for the formulation of the problems comes from practical activity. The problems are extra-scientifically formulated. But, disregarding the fact that the impulses for the research problems have extra-scientific origins, the decisive process direction runs from theory to practice. The procedure is that practical activity provides impulses for professional and sociopolitical considerations, which in their turn provide impulses for research. The production of knowledge is carried on to change social reality, to carry out the work of social change. First comes the systematic and scientific production of knowledge and then follows the work of social change. We can call this type of work *research for change*.

As we said above, Zimbalist identifies six central research themes in his survey of American research for change since the 1870s. These themes have also been, and still are, of interest in a European context. Some of the research reviewed by Zimbalist has its origins in British research, for example. Level of living studies in Sweden during the last two decades can by and large be regarded as research on the distribution and quantification of poverty, and 'indexing' in social work. Evaluation research is once again of interest as a consequence of economic crises in welfare states. If we consider these research themes on the basis of the criteria set up by Zimbalist for drawing up the boundaries between research in the work of social change (social work research, social welfare research), the problem of delimitation still remains.

From theory to practice – agent activity
In a previous section, I described the continuity in the history of ideas that runs from the historical theory of the Scottish school of thinkers through to the social change philosophies of history of the nineteenth century. The basic idea of these philosophies was that society was sick and would be cured by means of scientifically acquired knowledge. During the nineteenth century, several movements emerged that claimed to be able to change and improve society through scientific knowledge. In this connection, and without analysing them too deeply, it is usual to mention Saint-Simonism in France, The Fabian Society in England, and Verein für Sozialpolitik in Germany (see, for example, Frängsmyr 1980, Hirdman 1989). The Marxist movement with the Internationals in the forefront holds a special place in this context. Charles Fourier, who wrote about and tried to carry on the work of change through his campaigns, is one example of a single individual who fought a rather lonely battle to implement a philosophy of history in the nineteenth century.

Björn Eriksson points out that the question of which direction history would take was a core issue in the development of ideas in the nineteenth century. Different philosophies of history produced different answers. All agreed, however, that the sick society must be cured. Eriksson (1988:405) writes:

> *'It was not only Condorcet and Saint-Simon who tried to answer it. There was a succession of more or less well-known attempts at finding an answer. In these, and working from the idea of industrialism, they tried to build up the new world, a world freed from the poverty and misery that characterised the old one. Among these we must include Comte's Politique Philosophique from 1851, all of Fourier's writings on phalanstery, Proudhon's Philosophy of Poverty and so on. These were characterised by a repudiation of the world as it was at the same time as they accepted industrialism as the causally decisive phenomenon in the world they were trying to create, and knowledge as the method of coming to grips with social problems.'*

These authors' work and achievements are summarised as 'sociology as agent activity'.

> *Simply summarised, we can say that sociology exists as agent activity when a group of people with a theory on the future development of society want to speed up its change in this direction. This means that sociology as agent activity is made up of three disparate but interconnected elements: a theory of society and history; a programme for*

*changing society from a bad present situation to a good future one; and
a group of people who are committed to implementing this change'*
(Eriksson ibid).

In terms of the terminology that I use in this study, agent activity corresponds to
the 'from theory to practice' tendency in the history of ideas, which is the
theme of chapter 3. The tendency I describe here means that research, the
philosophies of history and the theoretical constructions form the basis and
starting point of programmes and action strategies for social practice, the work
of social change. In Björn Eriksson's study, this tendency is called 'sociology
as agent activity'. The central question is, of course, that of the relationship
between 'sociology as agent activity' and social work as 'the work of social
change', an issue that will be discussed in a later section.

From practice to theory

I have called the second tendency in the history of ideas 'from practice to
theory'. In terms of process thinking, it is practice, the work of social change,
that is primary and which forms the foundation for the compilation of knowledge.
Within this tradition, social work manifests itself mainly as a practical activity the
goal of which is to help people affected by social problems. Earlier in this study, I
wrote that one way of familiarising oneself with this tendency has been, and is, by
seeking social work's heritage of ideas in human sociality and mutuality in
giving help to one's fellow human beings. I claimed that this way of approaching the issue does not provide us with much guidance on understanding social
work as practice and as a scientific discipline. Sociality is a fundamental
feature of all human social existence. The concept can be compared with Johan
Asplund's (1987) 'social responsiveness', which has to do with people's basic
propensity to 'answer' when 'questions' are put to them. Social work as
practical activity and as scientific activity naturally has sociality included in it.
But social work as practical activity *and* as a scientific discipline, seen from the
'from practice to theory' perspective in the history of ideas, has its roots principally in the development of industrialism. The rapid industrialisation of
Europe and America with urbanisation, unemployment, shortage of housing,
and other social problems as consequences, activated people who wanted to
remedy what they considered to be problematic. Sometimes it is thought that
society generates social problems. Consequently something must be done
about the problem-generating society. But sometimes it is thought that it is the
individual that generates social problems, and this means that the action
strategy must be directed towards the problem-generating individual. Within
the framework of the 'from practice to theory' tendency, we find both of these

conceptions, which have developed in conflict with each other. Social work as practical activity develops both in Europe – especially in Great Britain where the industrial revolution originated – and in the United States. Developments in Britain provided impulses for developments in America, and vice versa.

After the American Civil War, the 'dependent classes', the poor, the mentally ill, and criminals, came more and more under the protection of the state administration. The care and control of these groups were gradually transferred to mental care institutions, prisons and state charity boards. Within the private sector, voluntary organisations and child care agencies began to grow. People engaged in both state and private charity work and, together with a number of intellectuals, organised the American Social Science Association (ASSA) in 1865. Soon it became apparent, however, that these two groups saw their interests differently. The intellectuals in ASSA considered that the primary aim was to develop and compile knowledge that could be used to change social problems. The practitioners, who worked with the care and control of the socially underprivileged, were, however, interested in developing immediate methods for care and control. Conflicts of interest became more serious. In 1874 the practitioners left ASSA and formed a new organisation, the Conference of Charities, which in 1879 was rechristened as the National Conference of Charities and Corrections (NCCC). This organisation is now known as the National Conference on Social Welfare (NCSW).

Germain and Gitterman (1980) point out that the ideological conflicts in the development of practical social work were more complex than the organisational changes. Several conflicting schools of ideas manifested themselves. There was even conflict within each ideological movement. The central controversial issue was about the origin of evil. Is it society or is it the individual that generates social problems?

During the 1880s, two professional groups developed in the United States: charity organisations and the settlement movement. Both movements spread relatively fast and their different ideologies had their origins in Victorian Britain. The movements also had different working methods. They attracted well-educated young people from the upper and middle classes, especially young women who, through their involvement, acquired social status and economic independence. Both movements had strong religious roots. Despite their different ideologies and working methods, both of these movements, The Settlement Movement and The Charity Organization Society, have had great influence on the development of social work.

Jane Addams and Mary Richmond were two important pioneers in these movements. Addams and her sympathisers settled in poor districts and lived side by side with the people who needed their help. The basic approach of The Settlement Movement was that it was the environment, that is society, that generated social problems, and that changes must be made in people's surroundings if we are to improve individuals' social situation and eliminate poverty. However, the Charity Organisation Society (COS), with Mary Richmond at the forefront, was not interested in social reforms. Their ideas were based on the fact that it was individuals themselves who were the cause of poverty and social problems.

One common feature shared by these two important movements in the history of social work is that they first develop as movements, as practice. Their social activity was naturally based on an understanding of the origins and character of social problems and insights into how they could be eliminated. But it was clear that the movements were born as social activities among people in need, and for them. They were not movements with their origins in strong and well-formulated research traditions or philosophies of history. It was not until later that they discovered the need to base social activity on systematic production of knowledge. This was expressed earlier and more clearly in the work of Jane Addams than that of Mary Richmond, even if the latter eventually wrote two of the classic method books of social work.

The Settlement Movement sought contacts with knowledge-producing institutions relatively early. There were personal contacts between Jane Addams and her colleagues on the one hand and prominent researchers involved in social issues such as John Dewey on the other. These contacts, and the wish of The Settlement Movement to establish a base for their practical social work in the production of knowledge, led to the founding of the Chicago School of Civics and Philanthropy, which in 1920 became the School of Social Service Administration at the University of Chicago (see further in Chapter 6).

Mary Richmond took a different attitude. In her striving to establish a base for casework through professional schooling, she was against university-based courses. She believed that it would ruin social workers' natural commitment to their work, and argued in favour of an independent school for training social workers. Through the COS in New York, the New York School of Philanthropy was established. It was later known as the New York School of Social Work and was incorporated into Columbia University in the 1940s.

The 'from practice to theory' tendency in the history of ideas in social work is a strong tradition. It is a tendency that first and foremost provides social work as practical activity with a historical identity. It also provides the profession with an identity. But what role does it play in relation to social work as a research tradition? Has it worked as a driving force for research in social work? And, if so, in what way? My hypothesis is that this tendency has meant very much to social work as a research tradition. The hypothesis can only be substantiated by means of a description of the history of ideas within the tendency.

Delimitation problems in social work
Social work as practical activity has points of contact with several neighbouring activities and professions. Psychologists, psychotherapists, nurses, lawyers, and policemen are examples of professions whose fields of work touch on or partly coincide with those of trained social workers. Social work as practical activity or as a profession develops side by side with these and other professions, and sometimes in competition with them.

Social work as a scientific discipline has points of contact with other disciplines such as sociology, psychology, law, and social politics. These disciplines lay claim to investigating different aspects of social life and claim that each and every one of them has its own specific object of study. In some cases, hybrids are formed between disciplines with the purpose of studying a common object of study – the sociology of law is one such example. Even social work itself has been perceived as a hybrid science. But as time has passed, the claims of social work to create an identity of its own as a research discipline in Sweden have become clearer and clearer. The professionalisation of social work is, of course, another important (external) factor.

That social work, sociology, psychology, and other disciplines claim to be specific research traditions depends on the specialisation that has taken place in the social and behavioural sciences. Both extra-scientific and intra-scientific reasons lie behind this tendency towards specialisation, which also involves fragmentation.

It should be emphasised that it was society's need to use the social sciences that contributed to a high degree to this specialisation. Several disciplines were involved as the basis for the education of a growing number of professions. During the nineteenth century, theoreticians searched for whole solutions to social problems or social change. In the twentieth century, the orientation has been towards solving limited problems through so-called 'piecemeal engineering' and this means that the demand for specialists, social workers among others, increased. But there were also other reasons for specialisation. The large number of new methods and theories developed to deal with increasing amounts of material and practical tasks was an important driving force behind specialisation (Liedman 1983).

Interdisciplinary (multidisciplinary, transdisciplinary) studies have been thought to be an antidote to the negative consequences of specialisation. But such attempts have, for several reasons, not proved very effective. One considerable obstacle is that the participating disciplines only contribute to the interdisciplinary research work with their own theory and method traditions.

Månsson (1990) has focused attention on the problem of fragmentation. Like many others, he regards the positivistic theory and method tradition as fragmenting, and finds parallels between the practice of social work and its knowledge base. Månsson argues that the qualitative theory and method tradition in social science is better suited to social work.

The question of the relationship between sociology and social work was referred to in an insidious way in an evaluation of Swedish sociology. The three Nordic sociology professors responsible for the evaluation write (Allard *et al* 1988:47):

> *'For disciplines without a theoretical tradition of their own and with no obvious international roots, noticeable identity problems arise. This is the case with social work. The most common solution has been that those working in the discipline stay within their original discipline in their research, but at the same time collaborate with other subjects. Most teachers of social work have also actively pursued their research activities in this way. The problem is that representatives of social work in the second generation risk being totally without the identity of a discipline and the theoretical core that connections to disciplines like sociology and psychology mean. This is perhaps why certain representatives of the discipline, among the professors mentioned above [Berglind, Sunesson, Swedner, and Börjeson], Harald Swedner ... devotes a great deal of energy to constructing a theoretical discipline identity of its own, or as he says a "field of content", for social work. This seems, however, to lead to artificial constructions and in the first place reinforces the scepticism felt when faced with the prospect of social work creating its own discipline identity that would remain constant at a minimum level over a period of time. It is reasonable to wonder whether or not social work as a university discipline should be linked much more strongly to both sociology and psychology than is the case at present. It is, on the other hand, important that social workers have opportunities of expressing their common interests as a professional body.*

I share the writers' opinion as far as the difficulties ascribed to social work are concerned, but I do not share their overall conclusion that social work should be incorporated into other disciplines so that it is ensured its own identity as a discipline at a minimum level of constancy over a period of time. I am of the opinion that Allardt, Lysgaard, and Bøttger Sørensen overrate the ability of sociology (and other social and behavioural science disciplines) to solve its theoretical and methodological problems, and underrate the ability of social work to develop a theoretical and methodological identity of its own.

It is true that sociology, since the Scottish school of writers, has developed both theory and method for analysis of society, and that the discipline has an established organisation as a result of a high degree of institutionalisation, among other things. There are many characteristics that underline the fact that sociology is an established discipline, both nationally and internationally. The discipline has developed many productive theories, thereby revealing important processes and mechanisms in society and social life, as well as a great number of practicable methods. But it is also true that the recurrent discussions about the discipline's theoretical core and methodological problems show that the discipline of sociology, *in principle*, is struggling with the same type of problems as social work as regards theories of science and knowledge. In a very interesting article in which he argues against Thomas Brante, the sociologist Björn Eriksson 1981:11) writes the following:

> '*Sociology has no examples whatsoever of such an amalgamation of empiricism and theory, where it is difficult to say where the boundary between them goes. They are on the whole totally independent of each other, something that is indicated by the usual comment on examination work: "perhaps you could try to push in a bit of theory somewhere as well". Sociology is characterised by the fact that its normal scientific work takes place within two traditions. One working field is a conceptually and theoretically oriented tradition that deals with abstract and overall social phenomena, often from a historical perspective. The other is a quantitative, investigative tradition that concentrates on more concrete phenomena, often in the context of the present situation. And these two traditions are, in the main, unconnected.*'

Another reason why the 'rescue' of social work does not require incorporation into other disciplines is that social work as a research discipline is not so lacking in traditions as may be thought. The main thesis of this book is that there are traditions in the history of ideas that social work can build on, and it is the aim of the book to provide empirical examples of traditions in ideas that can form a basis for the identity of social work as a scientific discipline.

As I see it, there are at least two central points of intersection between sociology and social work: one of them is their approach to social problems, and the other has to do with their approach to social change and the work of social change.

Let us first look at the connection between sociology and social work through the concept of social problem. Earl Rubington and Martin S Weinberg(1971:3-4) are the editors of a theoretically limited but often quoted book on sociology and social problems. The book starts from the following points:

'Clearly, there are social problems in modern society. There are also problems in their study. Some of the most basic of these are:

1. Who will study social problems?

2. What will they consider social problems?

3. Why will they study them?

4. How will they study them?

'Answers to these four questions emerged about seventy-five years ago in the United States with the development of sociology. Sociology deals with social interaction, those situations in which two or more people adapt their conduct to each other. Most social problems arise in the course of or in consequence of social interaction. Few of the developing disciplines in the late nineteenth century dealt with matters of this kind. Thus, partly by choice and partly by default, sociology appeared on the American scene to deal simultaneously with social problems and with social interaction.'

Rubington and Weinberg (ibid, p5) also write, and I think this is very interesting from the perspective of a history of ideas:

'The great bulk of the leading American sociologists were ministers' sons who had moved from small rural towns to the rapidly growing cities. They witnessed the changes from a farm to a factory economy. All about them they saw the signs of rapid change, its positive as well as its negative features. A philosophy of history that pointed toward moral progress guided their thinking. Yet at the same time they wished to

*improve the world in which they were living. Thus, on the one hand,
early American sociologists were more or less convinced that progress
and moral uplift would occur, yet, on the other hand, were concerned to
take a hand in solving some of the immediate problems of life in a
rapidly changing society. In dealing with the philosophy of history as it
had come down from the fathers of European sociology, American sociologists had begun to deal with the problems of their discipline. In
responding to their own reformist impulses they also began to deal with
the problems of society.'*

Rubington and Weinberg show how the study of social problems was such a
central issue for American sociology. This went hand in hand with studies of
what the authors considered another central object of study, namely social
interaction.

But the strong interest of sociology in studies of social problems does not only
concern American sociology. It also applies to a great extent to sociological
traditions where structural social mechanisms are the focus of attention, such
as Marxist sociology. For many sociologists, studies of social problems meant
that they also became involved in the practical work of social change.
American sociologists worked with piecemeal engineering, that is, reforms
involving small, step-by-step changes, while Marxists entered into political
action with system changes as their goal. Much later, the tradition of action
research was developed to combine sociological research with the practical work
of change.

In Sweden, Hans Berglind has focused attention on the approach of sociology
and social work to studies of social problems in an interesting way (1983).

Berglind's starting point is the idea that the discipline of social work is to study
the causes, consequences and treatment of social problems, and that these
studies are to be carried out at the society level, the intermediate (group) level
and the individual level. By using these variables, he constructs a field of characteristics with 9 cells. By means of an example about unemployment, he
illustrates how heavy the burden would be for social work if the discipline itself
were to carry out all the tasks involved.

Berglind thinks that such a research problem would be too comprehensive and
that, within the framework of the discipline, it is not possible to gain sufficient
knowledge in each and every one of the 9 cells. He points to the need to co-
operate with other disciplines, principally those of the social sciences.

*'As the subject is so extensive, an order of priorities must be set up between the different "cells". Since disciplines such as economics, sociology and social politics deal with the areas concerned in the upper three cells of the figure, **it may be appropriate** for the main emphasis in social work to be placed in **the lower right-hand corner** of the figure. It is, however, important that processes in the other cells are included as a background'* (Berglind 1983:24, emphasis added).

TABLE 2.1
Co-operation between social work and sociology: unemployment as an example
Source: Berglind (1983:24)

Problem Level	Nature and causes	Events and consequences	Treatment and action
Society (macro)	Economic competition Structural change ⟶	Regional and ⟶ business imbalance	Labour market policy
Community (meso)	Relocation Suburban environment ⟶	Social isolation Weakened ⟶ network	Community work Structure-oriented measures
Family Individual (micro)	Unemployment Family problems ⟶	Alcohol, drug abuse ⟶ Economic ⟵ problems	Treatment of family and individual

This shows how immediately and tangibly studies of social problems concern the areas of interest of sociology and social work. Rubington and Weinberg's standpoint is crystal clear when they write that what physics means to engineering, sociology means to social work.

Berglind is more cautious and considers it *appropriate* that social work occupies itself with individual and family treatment. A big problem with Berglind's suggestion is, if I understand it correctly, that cell 9, which comes under the column 'treatment and action', mainly deals with the practice of social work and not with its research. At best, this would involve research into treatment methods, which is problematical on account of the fact that knowledge generated is at a lower level of ambition (see further in chapter 7). Apart from this problem, there remains the question of assessing which of the two disciplines of sociology and social work is the most appropriate for different kinds of studies of social problems. This is an open question.

The other central point of intersection between sociology and social work concerns the approaches of these disciplines to social change and the work of social change. Both from the viewpoint of the history of ideas and by definition, attitudes towards social change and the work of social change are more controversial in sociology than in social work.

The task of contributing to and working with social changes is a built-in element in social work. In a certain sense, social work is the work of social change. It is because of this aspect of the discipline of social work that the two terms are used as synonyms in this book. We have already seen reasons for the convergence of these two terms. In the 'from practice to theory' tendency in the history of ideas, social work means quite simply the work of social change. All production of knowledge has its starting point in social work as social practice. In that sense, the work of social change is built into social work. The same type of phenomenon is present when we are dealing with the theoretical construction of the subject as a research discipline. When, for example, formulating a description of the professorships in social work, the work of social change is already built into the definition: 'Research within the field of the professorship should be organised in such a way that the results can be implemented in practical social work.'

Regardless of which tendency in the history of ideas is taken as a point of departure, it seems to be that the production of knowledge and the relationship of research to the work of social change is characterised by nearness and immediacy in the discipline of social work. Social changes are of natural concern to social work, and the work of social change is taken as something natural to aim for.

The relationship of sociology to social change and the work of social change, on the other hand, has always been more controversial, particularly as regards the latter. The various sociological traditions formulate different interests in knowledge and ascribe different roles to the researcher. Positivist sociology, for example, has adopted a technically manipulative interest in knowledge and seen the researcher's role as descriptive. Marxist sociology formulates its interest in knowledge as politically emancipatory and regards the researcher as a participant in the work of social change.

The early sociologists or social philosophers had a lot to say about what was right and wrong in society, but spoke very little about the role of sociology in the work of social change. The origins of American sociology, which are almost contemporary with the European classics, present another orientation for the social role of sociology. As I stated earlier, American sociologists were pragmatists; right from the beginning, sociology was interwoven with studies of social problems and with social reforms.

In modern times, there has been a debate on the social role of sociology between Alvin Gouldner (1961, 1973) and Howard S Becker, and this has since left its mark on sociologists' attitudes towards the work of social change. The debate had its starting point in Max Weber's (1977) well-known essays, 'Science as a Profession' and 'Politics as a Profession', in which Weber argues that we must distinguish between scientist and politician roles.

Another variant of this debate took place, especially in the late 1960s and early 1970s, between positivist sociology and the advancing Marxist sociology. The debate meant a criticism of the technically manipulative interest in knowledge of positivism (in Comte's terms 'Savoir pour prévoir, pour pouvoir'), and a plea for the emancipatory interest of Marxism in knowledge.

A theoretical frame of reference

Two central variables of different aspects of social work are brought out in this book: the first one is the development in the history of ideas in which the interplay between theory and practice acquires a prominent role. In this context, I have carved out two tendencies in the history of ideas; 'from theory to practice' and 'from practice to theory'.

Secondly, I want to illustrate the nature of the causes of social problems. Two polarised concepts manifest themselves: society generates social problems and the individual generates social problems. It is both possible and productive to carve out ideal-typical variable values, and consequently to dichotomise these two variables.

In my presentation, the two tendencies in the history of ideas have been refined with the aim of elucidating different working processes pursued by thinkers and practitioners. In reality, the relationship between theory and practice is complicated and constitutes one of the most central issues in the philosophy of science and theories of knowledge. It is not my task here to give an account of the most important standpoints in the philosophy of science.

If, for analytical purposes, we want to refine the relationship between theory and practice, we can only do so in terms of tendencies. I have thus used the concepts of 'from theory to practice' and 'from practice to theory' as tendencies. By the 'from theory to practice' tendency, I mean that research results and theoretical knowledge form the foundation of social practice, the work of social change.

I have here emphasised the primacy of theory and have wished to bring out its central role as a guide to the work of social change. But in so doing, I have not wished to detract from the role of practice in its interplay with theory within the framework of the prevailing tendency. The same goes for the 'from practice to theory' tendency, where social practice, the work of social change, forms the foundation for the production of theoretical knowledge.

The 'nature of causes of social problems' variable has also been dichotomised, in spite of the fact that we today are well aware that the causes of social problems are to be found at a number of 'levels', and that there exists a complicated and lively interaction between these multi-level causes. It is, however, prudent to refine and dichotomise this variable. If we look upon it from a history of ideas viewpoint, we see that thinkers and practitioners have thought and acted on the basis of the dichotomy 'society is sick' and 'the individual is sick'.

Those who have sought the causes of social problems in society have considered society to be sick. As pointed out earlier, this was a central idea among many nineteenth-century thinkers and systems builders. The systems builders often directed their efforts at total upheavals of society to develop better conditions of life for mankind. The most classical example is perhaps that of the Marxist analysis of society and revolutionary programme of change. But among those who considered that the causes of social problems were in society there was also an alternative strategy to the total changing of society. Social changes through reforms, partial changes, or 'piecemeal engineering' as the English philosopher Karl Popper (1957) put it, was the other strategy. During the twentieth century, references were gradually made to the 'environment', and by that they meant structural conditions in society.

The opposite view was to regard man as the source of social problems and to seek the causes in individuals themselves. Psychopathological or moral defects in the individual created social problems. In order to eradicate social problems, they thought, you had to cure the individual by means of psychiatric, psychological, and moral treatment methods. The variables chosen refer to two central, connected circumstances in the development of social science. The first variable, the interaction of theory and practice, refers ultimately to the knowledge-producing nature of the working process. In the interplay between theory and practice, we try to *explain* and *understand* social phenomena. When we consider that we have knowledge of a certain social phenomenon, whether by charting the causes that explain the phenomenon or through an understanding that alludes to the social meaning attributed to it, we can go one step further in the working process. This step consists in attempts to change social reality, which in its turn presupposes that we have a theory of what should be changed to achieve the desired effects. We can say that while the interplay between theory and practice has to do with the generation of knowledge in general, the nature of the causes of social problems deals with what specifically should or is to be changed in social life. In this way the two variables are linked together, which is also evident when reading the so-called classics of the social sciences.

A dichotomised cross-tabulation of the variables *development in the history of ideas of the interaction between theory and practice*, and the *nature of the causes of social problems*, with the variable values 'from theory to practice' and 'from practice to theory', as well as 'society generates social problems' and 'the individual generates social problems', produces the following four-field table:

The thinkers and practitioners who in one way or another are considered to belong to the classics and pioneers of social work can be placed in the different fields of the table. However, it is not my intention to include every conceivable classic and pioneer. The aim is to give examples that are considered typical of the fields of characteristics of the four-field table.

FIGURE 2.1 The theoretical frame of reference of the study

Nature of the causes of social problems

		Society generates social problems	The individual generates social problems
Development of ideas in the interaction between theory and practice	From theory to practice	1	2
	From practice to theory	3	4

Field 1 is characterised by developments in the history of ideas where the predominant tendency runs from theory to practice. Here the focus is on society as the generator of problems. 'Sociology as agent activity', Saint-Simonism, and Marxism are good examples of movements and traditions of thought that are placed in field 1.

Field 2 is characterised by a tendency in the history of ideas running from theory to practice. The causes of social problems are to be sought in the individual, who is considered to be problem-generating. In the social sciences, it is mainly psychological approaches that are located in this field of knowledge.

Field 3 is characterised by the predominance of the tendency from practice to theory, at the same time as the causes of social problems are to be sought in society. Jane Addams and The Settlement Movement are examples of pioneers who can be placed in this field.

In all three of these fields can also be placed what was called research for change in a previous section. Research for change really belongs to the upper part of the four-field table, especially to field 1. But against the background of external interaction between theory and practice in research for change, this type of research and practice in social work can be related to the lower half of the table, especially field 3.

Field 4 is characterised by the fact that the tendency from practice to theory is predominant, at the same time as the causes of social problems are to be found in the individual. A typical example is The Charity Organization Movement with Mary Richmond as the leading figure.

Summary
The purpose of this chapter has been to develop a theoretical frame of reference for studies and assessment of social work in the light of the history of ideas. My point of departure was that social work is a practical activity and a scientific discipline. Can the discipline be defined so precisely that its main area of work, its conceptual content and its historical traditions can be specified? It is apparent that there are many different types of definitions that can be applied to social work as a practical activity and as a scientific discipline. It is natural that different definitions can be provided since there is constant interplay between concepts and social phenomena. There is a dynamic character to what researchers and practitioners do in social work. The conceptual content of the discipline varies because research and the practical work of change are carried

on in different fields. The historical tradition of the discipline grows as time goes on, and therefore the choice of historical situation will be the decisive factor in choosing a definition. That social work has so many different definitions is thus a natural state of things. It is the task of a study of the history of ideas to discover the various definitions that have been given to the discipline.

Social work is also a practical activity, work of social change. The idea of *Homo ad juvendum paratus*, that is the human propensity to strive for mutual help and to be prepared to give help, is an important basis for social work. This fundamental human sociality has been laid as a foundation, and even as a criterion of determining the history of ideas in the discipline. Naturally, this point of departure has its value, but it cannot be productive if we understand social work as practice and as a scientific discipline. I claim that the description and analysis of the historical background of ideas to social work must be founded on the development of social science. This means that the development of social analysis in the western tradition of thought during the nineteenth century must be the first arena for digging up the roots of the history of ideas in social work. This development is followed by the prevailing nineteenth-century tendency towards the work of social change. What happened in the nineteenth century is of extremely central importance to social work. While developments in the history of ideas during the eighteenth century can be seen as preludes, it is the progress made in the nineteenth century that is the basis on which social work develops. The discipline of social work develops partly hand in hand with other disciplines, which gradually take on sharper contours in the process of specialisation in social science, and partly as a result of the practical work of social change. From this development there arise questions of crucial importance to the social legitimacy of the discipline: What is the discipline's identity? What are the boundaries of the discipline in relation to other disciplines?

In this chapter, I have dealt with the relationship of social work with sociology and pointed out two important points of intersection between these disciplines. In Chapter 5, I shall take up the relationship of the discipline with psychology on the basis of the concept of social casework.

As regards the relationship to sociology, I draw the conclusion that the problem of delimitation will remain for the unforeseeable future. This is because both sociology and social work partially lay claim to common areas of activity, both in their research work and in their work of social change. The present balance of power indicates that sociology is stronger as regards social theory and methods of analysis, whereas social work has its strength in its orientation towards the work of social change, which has always been the mainstay of the discipline's tradition.

The struggle for where the limits are to be drawn, and partly the division of labour between them, will be dependent on how each discipline develops. How they develop is an open question. In this struggle, the uncovering of the discipline's links to the classics of social science is an important research task. Classics are classics because they have a message for society of today. An important mission for the discipline of social work is to root itself in the classics of social science and thereby create a more-clear-cut identity for itself.

It is with this purpose in mind that the frame of reference is intended to be used. The frame of reference is based on two variables which, in the perspective of the history of ideas, play a central role in the development of social science disciplines. The interplay between theory and practice, and views of the nature of the causes of social problems are central themes among the classics.

Establishing a base for the history of ideas in social work in the classics of social science can be done by using the frame of reference to classify and assess thinkers and practitioners. In this way, we can clarify similarities and differences between the classics, which is also a means of elucidating issues that form a field of tension in social work. The frame of reference is intended to be used to (1) classify classical thinkers and practitioners to identify similarities and differences between them, and to study lines in the history of ideas that lead to modern thinking on social work and (2) justify why certain classics may be judged to be the classics of social work. The frame of reference is thus intended to be used for the purpose of *generating hypotheses* in the research process.

Chapter 3
Saint-Simonism and Social Work

'... *few movements in the intellectual history of nineteenth-century France have had as momentous and varied an impact on the development of social philosophy of that century as has Saint-Simonism. The conception of society as an organic whole subject in all its aspects to social law, a view which they shared with August Comte and Henri de Saint-Simon, was to dominate French sociological thought through Durkheim.*'

(George G Iggers 1958)

Introduction
In chapter 2, I developed a theoretical frame of reference to make it possible to systematise the development of the history of ideas in social work. This frame of reference is based on two central variables of the different aspects of social work. The first variable has to do with the interaction of theory and practice, while the second expresses the nature of the causes of social problems. The first variable reveals two fundamental tendencies in the history of ideas. The one line of development goes 'from theory to practice', where theoretical knowledge forms the starting point and basis of practice or work of social change. The second line of development goes 'from practice to theory' and means that practice or work of social change constitutes the starting point and basis of theoretical knowledge and development of knowledge. The second variable deals with the nature of the causes of social problems and is intended to capture conceptions in the literature which are predominantly to do with the history of ideas. With regard to this variable, two variable values have been carved out: 'society generates social problems' and 'the individual generates social problems'.

A cross-tabulation of these two dichotomised variables produces an area of characteristics with four fields. One of these fields characterises thinkers, social analysts and practitioners who belong to the history of ideas tendency 'from theory to practice', and who seek the causes of social problems in society. It is in this field that Saint-Simon's social philosophy occupies a central place, and it is this which is the focus of this chapter.

During the sixteenth century, a number of books were published about Utopias. The word comes from the Greek 'a topos' and means 'the land which is nowhere'. Utopia stood for the idea of a better society and a better life, in contrast to the problems and misery of the society in which people lived. The inspiration

47

for sixteenth-century strivings to formulate Utopias originated in the classics of ancient Greece and Rome. As early as the beginning of the fourteenth century, a number of scholars in Italy, later called humanists, had rediscovered the classical idea of a better life, free from social problems. The primary task of the humanists was to restore the most central and useful principles of the Ancient Classical World and then apply them to contemporary Renaissance society. These thinkers and scholars started to lay the foundations of the notion of 'progress'. 'Striving for progress' or 'the spirit of human progress' was to do with people's willingness to improve their living conditions. During the eighteenth century, when the concept became fully developed, what they meant was people's potential ability to control their physical environment and social surroundings if they, instead of using magic, used their reason to discover the laws governing nature and developed the scientific techniques required to make the best use of nature.

The American historian Sheldon J Watts (1984:10-11) writes in his book *A Social History of Western Europe 1450-1720*:

> '*Already in the 1620s intellectuals of the calibre of Sir Francis Bacon, Lord Chancellor of England, had arrived at the startling conclusion - anticipated by Aristotle in the fourth century BC - that the material world could not be altered by invoking demons, using magical rituals or commanding changes to be made in physical objects through intensive concentration of the faith moveth mountains variety. Instead, Bacon and men like him perceived that man's mastery over Nature could be achieved by establishing causal connections between relevant pieces of matter and using these materials in accordance with the universal laws of Nature which learned men such as Copernicus and Galileo had already begun to discover.*
>
> *. . . for his part, Bacon concluded that by bringing together the theories supplied by learned scholars with the practical empirical knowledge supplied by artisans and craftsmen like those who had cobbled together the compass, the first printing press and gunpowder, humankind could gain mastery over their material environment and for the first time in human history abolish hunger, poverty and ignorance.*'

Watts's purpose is to bring out Bacon's insight into the fact that researchers' theories and practitioners' tested experience could, and must, be used in the field of natural science in order for man to be able to be in control of the material world.

It was to take some time before these ideas could be applied within the field of social sciences. The analysis of society was put on a scientific footing with the Scottish writers in the mid-eighteenth century. An understanding of the fact that social science and analysis of society could, and should, be used to control and improve the social environment was first manifested in de Condorcet's *Esquisse* from 1793. de Condorcet also had a French social tradition to lean back on: demands for reform pointing in various directions evolved in France in the middle of the eighteenth century. Those groups that for various reasons fought for influence at the court were at the same time groups through which the interests of wider classes of society could be expressed in the central circles of the nation. Physiocracy is one such social movement in these conflicts between different factions. It is both an economic as well as a political and social reform movement. 'If we were to give this movement (which had no name and no unified organisation) a name, we could call it the reform bureaucrats' (Elias 1939).

The thinker who first developed this line, and who formulated how the analysis of society could be used in work of social change, was Claude Henri de Rouvroy, Comte de Saint-Simon. This is my main reason for choosing to present Saint-Simon and Saint-Simonism to illustrate one of the several roots of the history of ideas in social work.

Yet another reason is that, despite the fact that the Saint-Simonists were primarily interested in Saint-Simon's programme for action and not in his analysis of society, Saint-Simon and Saint-Simonism can be regarded as a whole consisting in three parts: a theory of society and history; a programme of action to eliminate the evils of society; and a group of people who took it upon themselves to be the agents of change. It is therefore a question of a package in which theory, a programme of action, and agents of change are included. Modern social work, in contrast with other social science disciplines, has a clear-cut ambition of providing such packages for the work of social change.

A third reason for my choice of Saint-Simon is that he is the first bridge-builder who comprehensively spans the analysis of society that evolved during the eighteenth century and the efforts of the nineteenth century to use this analysis of society to remedy the evils of society.

It is thus my intention in this chapter to investigate Saint-Simon's and Saint-Simonism's social philosophy as one of the foundations of the roots of the history of ideas in social work.

The questions at issue which are discussed in this chapter comprise the following main points: What were the main features of Saint-Simon's social philosophy? As a social and history of ideas phenomenon, in what does Saint-Simonism consist? What is the nature of the connection between Saint-Simon's thinking and development models for modern social work? And in that case, in what do these elements consist? Is it possible to find models similar to Saint-Simon's thinking and to Saint-Simonism in the way Swedish social policy has evolved? In what way can the welfare work of the 1930s and 1940s, and the work done in commissions of inquiry in the 1970s which led up to the 1982 Social Services Act, illustrate this line running from Saint-Simon to modern social work? Why can, and why should, social work be rooted in a classic such as Saint-Simon?

After this introduction, I shall, in the next section, present Saint-Simon's and Saint-Simonism's social philosophy as a history of ideas phenomenon. These sections are relatively detailed, and my motivation for this is that it has not been usual to present Saint-Simon and his successors in connection with social work. In this chapter I pursue the thesis that there are elements of thought running from Saint-Simon to modern social work in Sweden, and that this consists in an inheritance of ideas from Saint-Simon and Saint-Simonism. I illustrate this thesis by means of two development phases in Swedish welfare work. Firstly I shall use the historian Yvonne Hirdman's study of how welfare work developed in Sweden during the 1930s and 1940s. The focus here is on the work of Gunnar and Alva Myrdal. I shall then use the work of the commissions of inquiry which forms the basis of the 1982 Social Services Act. I shall study the aims and methods of the social services and illuminate these from the viewpoint of their inheritance from Saint-Simon and Saint-Simonism.

Saint-Simon's thinking
Claude Henri de Rouvroy, Comte de Saint-Simon, 1760-1825, belonged to the French aristocracy and lived during a troublesome political period in France. One of his first teachers was D'Alembert, a co-author of the well-known *Encyclopédie*. As was the family tradition, Saint-Simon joined the French armyand fought in America during the American Revolution. On returning home, he decided not to take part in the French Revolution, which was then in progress.In this way he managed to survive even the most dangerous periods of it. He made a large fortune through shady business deals and speculation. When the Revolution was over, he established himself as a 'grand seigneur', a noble gentleman, and devoted himself to higher education. Saint-Simon managed to gather around him the learned men of the time. He was very generous to those

around him, but his wealth ran out and he was forced to make a living by working as an assistant in a pawnbroker's. He lived partly on the support of a man who had previously been one of his servants. During this period he did his writing in the evenings and finished one of his first great works. His family, who tired of his way of life, started paying him a pension in 1814. He once again gathered intellectuals around him. For a time the great historian Augustin Thierry was his secretary. August Comte, who is sometimes called the father of sociology, worked for him for a time as well. Saint-Simon's radicalism deeply troubled both his family and other aristocrats. His pension was withdrawn. In desperation he tried to commit suicide. From 1823 up to his death in 1825, Saint-Simon was supported by his adepts, who admired him and even declared him a genius.

Saint-Simon's life was full of ups and downs. He was not alone in this, however. He belonged to a group of people of intellectual and Bohemian lifestyle. Other known personalities in this connection were Diderot and Comte. Albert Salomon (1955) describes these thinkers as 'bohemian Messiahs'.

During his lifetime, Saint-Simon was relatively unknown as a social thinker. Most of his writings were published posthumously, often as selected works. *Oeuvres de Saint-Simon et d'Enfantin*, (Paris: Dentu 1865-1876, and Paris: Leroux 1877-1878) comprises 47 volumes. Saint-Simon's writings are in volumes 15, 18-23 and 37-40. There are also other publications: *Oeuvres complétes de Saint-Simon* (1832) and *Oeuvres de Saint-Simon* (1841), published by O Rodrigues; *Oeuvres choisis de C H Saint-Simon* (1859), published by C Lemonnier. The writings are mainly available in French, but some are reproduced by later writers in English translation. The most extensive is *Henri, Comte de Saint-Simon: Selected Writings* by F M H Markham (1952).

Shortly after his death, a group of people took the initiative to start a social movement which was later to be called Saint-Simonism. The Saint-Simonists made their own interpretations of Saint-Simon's analysis and philosophy of society, and were most interested in his programme for social change. Saint-Simon's scientific discussion had a strong influence on August Comte, thought by many to be the father of modern sociology. Emile Durkheim, whose analysis of society is still an important source of inspiration for modern sociology, was also influenced by Saint-Simon's theories.

Saint-Simon's thinking constitutes an analysis of society and a philosophy of history. The latter resulted in thoughts on how sick society could be cured, and this became a sort of model for change. Saint-Simon had a clear idea of the social structure of society. He considered that the class structure consisted in 'the productive' and 'the non-productive' social groups. Financiers, industrialists, scientists and workers belonged to the productive group. Saint-Simon expounded an interesting theory on the historical development of society. This development was for Saint-Simon identical to that of scientific knowledge. Scientific knowledge and rationality were the only means of explaining and understanding social phenomena in general and social problems in particular. Social systems were created, developed, and eventually disappeared, according to Saint-Simon. There was always a struggle between the old and the new, and a period of transition between the disappearing social system and the one being born.

Durkheim (1928:118-119) characterised Saint-Simon's conception of historical change as being organic and full of conflict in the following way:

> *'In the measure that the ancient social system gave way, another was formed in the very bosom of the first. The old society contained within itself a new society, in process of formation and every day acquiring more strength and consistency. But these two organizations are necessarily antagonistic to each other. They result from opposing forces and aim at contradictory ends. One is essentially aggressive, war-like, the other essentially pacifist.'*

Saint-Simon saw the fundamental problems of society as a consequence of an imperfect concordance between formal and real power in society. The industrialists were the driving force in society, that is, they had informal power but lacked the formal power which would have made it possible for them to influence society and bring about better order without any social problems. It is at this stage that Saint-Simon launches his programme for social change. Saint-Simon's programme of action envisaged both organisational changes and changes of attitudes and values. The organisational changes would put formal power in the hands of the bearers of knowledge, as these were considered best suited to plan, organise and lead society. Saint-Simon proposed a parliament consisting of three chambers: 'Chambre d'invention', 'chambre d'examen', 'chambre d'exécution'. The first chamber was to be made up of people who could come up with ideas and show what the future of society could be like. In this group were included actors, musicians and painters for example. The second chamber was to be constituted of scientists who would decide how society was to be organised. The third chamber was to consist of men from the world of industry and commerce who were strong enough to act. The industrialists would plan and control society according to the knowledge, laws and organisations developed by the scientists.

It was scientific knowledge that was the most important element in Saint-Simon's analysis of society. The evolution of knowledge, the genesis and rise of the industrial society, the Protestant revolution, and the Age of Enlightenment all contributed to the fall of medieval society. Saint-Simon maintained that the evolution of knowledge went through three stages: theological, metaphysical, and scientific. He regarded studies of human society as a positive science which he called 'social physiology'. His belief in the power of science, and especially that of social science, to free society of social problems bordered on over-confidence in those powers. He thought that the religious educated élite of the Middle Ages would be replaced by a new, international scientific and industrial élite. Science would replace religion.

In his earlier works, Saint-Simon had emphasised the central role of science in the work of social change. In his later works, an idea of a new spirit began to manifest itself. This thought was not entirely new, however, as it can also be found in his earlier works. But it is in the later works that 'the new religion' is developed. Saint-Simon considered that the new society, which through its new organisation would eliminate social problems, must also undergo a spiritual change. New values and attitudes would change and unite people. Saint-Simon wrote about a new religion, 'Le Nouveau Christianism'. The question of social spirit, or the need for a spiritual change, later became a tradition that strongly influenced coming generations of social analysts. The new religion would create a new spirit in society – the society towards which all social forces and social tendencies were oriented. This trend in French social analysis can be seen again in almost identical form in the work of the ageing Comte, and it returns in a changed state in Durkheim, firstly as social solidarity in his early works and then as an almost religious feeling in the late *Vie Religieuse* (Eriksson1988).

Another interesting aspect of Saint-Simon's thinking is its internationalism (Zeitlin, 1968). The transition to the new cannot, in the opinion of Saint-Simon, be realised in a society isolated from other countries. The countries of Europe have similar historical, cultural, religious and economic backgrounds, which means that what happens in one country has consequences for the others. Saint-Simon thought that changes in society aimed at improving the state of things, and at eliminating what were considered to be social problems, presupposed that the educated masses in different countries became involved and co-operated with one another. He was not only convinced of the necessity of internationalism but also of the destructive power of nationalism. He perceived patriotism as national egoism, and this was a basis of antagonism between different nations.

The importance of internationalism to social changes is a central recurring theme in many nineteenth- and twentieth-century scientists and practitioners. This theme, which recurred in both theoretical and empirical works, as well as in considerations of a practical/political nature, is to be found in Karl Marx's social philosophy and social analysis. As we shall see in chapter 6, Jane Addams and The Settlement Movement also had internationalism as an important theme in social work.

Saint-Simon's fundamental concepts

Saint-Simon's analysis of society and his thinking comprise some central concepts which were handed down not only to the Saint-Simonists but also to other traditions. Before I move on to how the Saint-Simonists managed their inheritance from Saint-Simon, it would perhaps be appropriate to summarise some of the concepts central to Saint-Simon's thinking.

Society is sick. A very central element in Saint-Simon's social philosophy is that society is sick. In the terminology of his time it was natural to regard society as 'sick', a metaphor which later disappeared from the lexicon of social science. The social problems which befell people had their causes in the mechanisms of society, and not in the individual, as other thinkers were later to claim. The structure of society, the balance of power, the lack of concordance between real and formal power in society, constituted the basic causes of social problems. Saint-Simon regarded it as his primary mission to save mankind from a sick society.

Science will cure the sick society. Science, claimed Saint-Simon, was the principal instrument for curing society. It is also important to point out that the use of science with the aim of curing the sick society was an unknown theme in the eighteenth century. But during the nineteenth century, this became a theme very central to the growing scientific traditions and to social philosophies. With Saint-Simon, science made its definite entrance in the service of society. That science should be, and is, the central instrument in the hands of those who wish to change society for the better became the predominant way of thinking among social scientists, particularly those who consider themselves to belong to the positivist tradition.

The organised authority. Saint-Simon was convinced that the elimination of social problems required a new social organisation in which formal power was given to the bearers of knowledge, as these were best suited to plan, organise and lead society. The new social organisation was an organisation of the authority in society.

The total organisation of people's lives. This concept is closely linked to the idea that science will cure the sick society, and that the authority (scientific knowledge and rationality) is organised in the way described by Saint-Simon. The individual was to be subordinate to the collective, that is to say the collective that expressed itself in the form of organised authority.

Saint-Simonism: the agents
Saint-Simonism was a social movement which claimed to be Saint-Simon's heirs. The movement did not arise until after Saint-Simon's death and existed for a brief but intensive period.

Shortly after Saint-Simon's death, a group of people began to call themselves Saint-Simonists. Some of them belonged to the small group that Saint-Simon had gathered around him during his later years. Others had only met him, but had not necessarily belonged to Saint-Simon's group. After only about a year, the movement went into a romantic, visionary phase in which they tried different ways of living which on the whole were similar to modern attempts to develop alternative ways of life in local society. This phase came to an end at the beginning of the 1830s, and the movement gradually became a religious society that lived its own life and finally disappeared during the 1860s.

Saint-Simon's bequest implied above all an analysis of society and a social philosophy that contained guidelines on how the sick society could be cured with the help of science. The Saint-Simonists regarded themselves as Saint-Simon's heirs and as agents of change who would improve society. In the modern sense, social workers are experts, professional *agents of change*, who base their actions on scientific knowledge. The Saint-Simonists were not professional in the same sense. The time was not ripe for that, and Saint-Simonism was a far too parenthetical phenomenon to be able to develop professionalism. The essence of Saint-Simonism showed, however, elements of professionalism. The main signal was that work of social change should be based on Saint-Simon's analysis of society.

The Saint-Simonists, with people like Olinde Rodriguez, Barthélemy-Prospèr Enfantin, and Saint-Amand Bazard in the foreground started in 1826 the flagship of the movement, the periodical *Le Producteur, journal philosophique de l'industrie, des sciences et des beaux-arts*. The ideas propagated by this journal were those inherited from Saint-Simon. Society was considered sick. Science would solve the problems, and the fine arts would state the objectives of civilised society. Saint-Simon's ideas on the organisation of formal power in the new society would be put into practice. Internationalism was still one of the mainstays. Industrial development and scientific knowledge were by their nature international and not limited by national borders.

To begin with, *Le Producteur* contained the lines of thought inherited from Saint-Simon. This can also be seen in the journal's manifesto, in which the remedying of human problems is carried out with the help of a 'positive' method:

> *'The journal which we are announcing has as its purpose the develop-*
> *ment and dissemination of principles for a philosophy of the nature of*
> *man, and the recognition that it is the task of mankind to investigate and*
> *change the environment to its own benefit. The means by which this aim*
> *will be achieved are to be found in man's physical, intellectual and moral*
> *powers. Finally we emphasise that man's work to achieve this aim*
> *follows the increase in progress made'* (Charléty 1931:32).

Le Producteur propagated a model of change that was not completely clear in its outlines. It put forward three central principles which were, for all that, not exactly the same as those inherited from Saint-Simon.

The first principle is that social progress was dependent on the organised authority. The implementation of the good society, that is the curing of the sick society, required collective action. For the sake of the whole, the parts must make sacrifices. Individuals must subordinate themselves to the social order. This was to be achieved by 'l'éducation general', that is a general education based on a concept of what was good and what was bad in society. George Iggers (1958), an authority on Saint-Simon, was of the opinion that the Saint-Simonists' doctrine attempted to integrate the conservative tendency to utilise hierarchic organisations and authority with socialist values such as equality, and social and economic planning, for the best of man and society. In this way, they wanted to create a sort of authoritarian welfare state which would provide for its citizens.

The Saint-Simonists therefore regarded the liberal-humanistic idea of the autonomy of the rational individual as a negative force. The movement was a devoted advocate of the idea of total social organisation. This is a theme I shall return to in sections that follow.

The second principle of interest is dependent on the first. The Saint-Simonists strongly emphasised the fact that society must be controlled with love. Authority and love were two principles that were connected and which complemented one another. People must unconditionally subordinate themselves to authority.

But authority must guide people with love and devotion. A society controlled with authority but without love risked, and was even doomed to, ruin. We also find the principle of love in Saint-Simon, but it can be seen more clearly in the Saint-Simonists' model of action. Here it was action that was the primary thing. They had formed a movement to change the sick society. The new society must be characterised by a morality of love, rivalry between rich and poor must end, and there must be agreement between workers and decision-makers.

The third principle which distinguishes the Saint-Simonists from Saint-Simon himself was that they abandoned the idea of science and technology as the main remedies for the sick society. Instead they gradually went over to a religious: political solution to the problems of society. Their idea of the organised authority and religious devotion naturally went hand in hand.

Religious devotion was a feature inherited from Saint-Simon, especially from his later works. The new social spirit, or the new Christianity, was no substitute for science for Saint-Simon. With the Saint-Simonists, science was replaced by the new religion. This transition was connected with the fact that the social order would be propagated by means of a general education of the citizens. This general education would inform people of what was good and what was bad. The question was who would show the way and decide what was good and bad. The key was to find the best expert on the social order. Social order took on an almost holy nature and was connected with God.

During this period of change some institutional changes had also taken place. *Le Producteur* had been discontinued. The distribution of power within the group had been made clear. Most important of all, they had chosen two *Pères* (fathers) who were to determine what was good and bad in society. Father Enfantin and Father Bazard thus held the highest power in the movement, which had several hundred members. The movement acquired its own house in La Rue Monsigny in Paris, and was transformed into a religious movement. Enfantin and Bazard disagreed, however, on various issues. The conflict between them was resolved by the death of Bazard in 1831. Enfantin, who had taken on the role of prophet, became the sole leader and could play the part of the Messiah undisturbed. Saint-Simonism entered its last phase and lingered out its days. The movement was no longer a group of agents who would change the sick society on the basis of Saint-Simon's analysis of it and model of action. It lost its purpose and was overshadowed. The movement was dissolved when Enfantin died in 1864. There were some Saint-Simonists left after Enfantin's death, but they could hardly hold the movement together.

Saint-Simonism and modern social work

Saint-Simon's thinking and Saint-Simonism form a whole, comprising a theory of society, a programme of action for remedying the ills of society, and a group of people who have taken upon themselves the task of being agents of change. The main features of Saint-Simon and Saint-Simonism are shown in the diagram below.

FIGURE 3.1   Main features of Saint-Simon's thinking

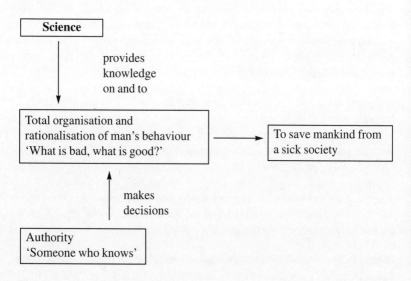

The diagram shows that society is considered to be sick and shall be cured. The curing of society is the goal to be achieved. Saint-Simon was very explicit in this respect, and expressed himself, among other ways, as follows: 'Gentlemen, I have only one passion – to make Europe peaceful; an idea – to reorganise European society' (Charléty 1931:10). The main instruments to be used to achieve the goal are science, the total organisation of society, and the authority.

It is the task of science to analyse society and to provide knowledge on its condition. Scientific knowledge will provide a basis for a total organisation of society and for the rationalisation of man's behaviour. The total organisation is decided by an authority who possesses great knowledge. But the authority must decide with love. Finally, the process of change is dependent on an international environment, since every society also depends on, is influenced by and influences, neighbouring societies.

It is in this way that Saint-Simonism's theory and practice are shaped. The new social analyst is not only a participating observer but also a participating agent of change. Durkheim (quoted by Salomon 1955:41) wrote as follows about the new role of the growing social science, 'sociology', in Saint-Simon:

> *'Saint-Simon saw clearly that his work would be a response and challenge to the Encyclopédie of the eighteenth century. The old Encyclopédie was critical and destructive. His own work would be constructive and integrative. He planned to build a systematic organization of all the sciences for the practical use of reorganizing society. For this reason, philosophy and what Comte was to call "sociology" were merging in a new pattern which was **theory and practice** at the same time. The new philosopher was not only a participant observer, but simultaneously a participant agent.*

> *'In other words, Saint-Simon was completely aware of the fact that he proposed a new approach to philosophy. The philosopher is, at his peak,\contemplative, but his thoughts are fruitful only if he is not merely the disinterested observer, but shares, with sympathetic understanding, in the grandeur and misery of society in its specific moments. Thus Saint-Simon is deeply convinced that from now on every philosophical system should and would be a social system'* (emphasis added).

The tradition whose main features were formulated by Henri de Saint-Simon was later given the name of 'sociology' by August Comte. The type of sociology developed by Saint-Simon and his successors is called 'sociology as agent activity'. My thesis is that, regardless of what the new type of social scientific analysis and practice are called, there is a tradition of thought which runs from Saint-Simon to modern social work. This tradition of thought consists mainly in the elements formulated by Saint-Simon. In that sense, 'sociology as agent activity' is also the developing 'social work as a discipline and practice'.

This history of ideas inheritance can be exemplified by means of various phenomena in the growth and development of modern welfare and social work. I shall describe two phases in the development of the Swedish welfare society. One is the development work undertaken during the 1930s and 1940s to build up a rationally planned welfare society in order to create 'the greatest possible happiness and the least possible unhappiness'. Here I shall use mainly Yvonne Hirdman's study *Att lägga livet till rätta - studier i folkhemspolitik* (1989). I take the other example from the work done during the 1970s in developing the new Social Services Act, which since 1982 has formed the basis of today's social work in Sweden. The material on which I base this example is taken from the reports of the Commission of Inquiry into the Social Services.

Saint-Simonism and Swedish welfare policy

Hirdman's study describes and analyses a number of phenomena in Swedish social policy and welfare work. One of her central themes of interest to us here is the connection she makes between the so-called Utopians and Swedish welfare work during the 1930s and 1940s. She presents her thesis as follows:

'My thesis is that these social reform programmes and their built-in, at times invisible norms, are far from being self-evident. In reality they have been governed by a clearly utopian intention, that is to say their ideological density was far greater than that presented by their unproblematic view of themselves and by the historical description that followed. There has been (is?) a purely utopian idea about the possibility (and duty) of rationally planning society in order to create the greatest possible happiness and the least possible unhappiness. With that I have also stated how I interpret the word utopia: planning as a means of achieving social harmony and happiness, where harmony and happiness are proposed from above as being irrefutably self-evident' (Hirdman, 1989:10).

Welfare work comprised, among other things, housing, family allowances, maternity benefits, child upbringing, home conditions, and lifestyles. In her introduction Hirdman quotes from the final report of the Population Commission in 1938 and from the Home and Family Inquiry of 1947. I reproduce these quotations as they clearly show the framework of the growing welfare work.

'It has been obvious during the work of the Population Commission that society, by means of socio-political measures, can do a great deal to put life right for the multi-child families of small means.

'It is a matter of explaining which home organisation is rationally justified in our time, and of arranging this so that the homes will be able to provide a solid framework for daily life, the space for an individually designed outer environment which man needs just as much now as before.'

Welfare work would be designed and developed by the social engineers. On the basis of scientific knowledge, it was their task to remedy what was considered undesirable, unfortunate and even unhealthy in society, and to create a better society – the so-called 'folk-home', the welfare society. There are striking similarities between the description of the art of social engineering presented by Alva Myrdal, one of the great social engineers of the 1940s, and the Saint-Simonism model.

*'[The social engineers] must now move from the mere registration of facts and the analysing of causal connections to the **drawing up of rational plans for appropriate changes**. Such a constructive piece of engineering art is in fact more reasonable in Sweden than in any other country. The underlying scientific theory, that a system of relevant value premises, together with a system of observed facts, is being applied, has actually been tested in Sweden'* (Alva Myrdal quoted by Hirdman 1989:12. Emphasis added).

To develop her thesis, Hirdman goes through the so-called Utopians of the nineteenth century and their ideas of the future, good society. She continues her presentation by introducing the Swedish Utopians. The development of welfare ideology and the advance of the 'social engineers' then form the background to the welfare work of the Myrdals and others in Sweden. Hirdman presents the Saint-Simonists, Charles Fourier's phalansterian society, Robert Owen's visions of a better society, and the feminist movement developed on the basis of Owen's ideas. Hirdman also briefly mentions the ideas of the so-called scientific Utopians, Karl Marx and Friedrich Engels.

The Utopians presented by Hirdman all propose future societies of different form and content. What unites them, however, is that Utopia stands for the positive as the opposite of the negative they themselves live in. Utopia will be freedom from the evil or the sick in society. And all these thinkers are, naturally, driven by the conviction that man has the ability to control the physical and social environment, the thought of 'the spirit of human progress'.

Yvonne Hirdman also shows that there were influential Swedish Utopians. One of them was Nils Herman Qviding, whose ideas influenced Hjalmar Branting and the Swedish labour movement. Qviding, born 1808, was a politician and writer who wanted to create an equal society in which the position of the upper class was reduced to the level of other classes. He thus advocated equalisation between the upper class and the lower class; equalisation also concerned the relationship between the state and local government. Hirdman is of the view that Qviding regarded self-government as a prerequisite of class equality. He planned a Utopian society that would include the whole of Europe. All European societies would be under one state. Under the state would be the nations, under the nations the countries, under the countries the counties, and under the counties the districts. 5,000 people would live in each district. In Nils Herman Qviding's society there would above all be equalisation of the classes. He also gave his views on love, women, child upbringing, and so on. Hirdman points out that Qviding's Utopia was inspired by Plato as well as by Fourier and Owen.

At the same time, his thoughts were centred on Swedish poverty. Qviding, according to Hirdman, wanted to use poverty as a means of legitimising his Utopia, his ideas of charity and his patriarchal outlook. Qviding's undemocratic supremacy was expressed in the design of his Utopian society, in which cleaning patrols and watchmen for the maintaining of inner order were self-evident features.

Nils Herman Qviding was not the only one to put forward ideas about a future society, free from evil. People like Axel Danielsson, one of the leading figures of the labour movement, Erik Hedén, Hinke Bergegren and Frida Steenhof were other personalities who meant a lot to the development of welfare work during the growth of the Social Democratic movement. Ellen Key was another central figure in this connection. Key had a so-called home Utopia in which children were the most important target. The tasteful and clean home was the place where you could distinguish between good and bad tastes, and was where you could teach this to the children. By force of her nature, it was the woman who was ruler of the home, and this gave her special qualities for caring for, and bringing up, the children, according to Key. What Hirdman writes about Key's conception of man shows clear similarities with the notion of man that dominated Saint-Simon's thinking. I quote Hirdman (1989:86):

> *'If, behind ideas about male and female, we can discern a common*
> *notion of man in Ellen Key, it was the view of the liberal social reformer.*
> *It was an approach from above, which drew its knowledge of man from*
> *Darwinian biology, from the expanding field of medicine, and from*
> *physics and chemistry. We could call it a "veterinary view". It was*
> *basically the same view of man that the utopians also held: people were*
> *formable and full of almost divine qualities. . . Doctors and veterinary*
> *surgeons therefore pleaded (often passionately) that people should at*
> *least be treated like animals: see to it that they had an acceptable place*
> *to live, that they were not cold, that they got nourishing food.*
>
> *'It was this veterinary view that made the radical liberals attempt to direct*
> *the invisible hand by legislation for the protection of people's health and*
> *well-being.'*

With the contributions of Alva and Gunnar Myrdal to the social debate, the Utopian images began to take on a rationalistic character. By force of their scientific competence, the Myrdals came to symbolise the art of social engineering during the 1930s and 1940s. The Myrdals put forward their research results and ideas on welfare work, and the role of science in the creation of the good society, in a number of articles and in their ground-breaking book *Kris i befolkningsfrågan*, which was published in 1934.

The art of social engineering brought together science, economics, technology, and politics. This combination lent strength to politics. Gunnar Myrdal saw social life and its problems as the illogical result of historical evolution. But it was possible for people to determine themselves how this development could be changed. It was scientific knowledge and the techniques that had been developed which constituted the means of determining historical development. Scientific knowledge would free people from dangerous politics. The state stood for good politics. In a publication from 1967, Gunnar Myrdal developed and elucidated his thoughts on the interplay of scientific rationality with the role of the good (welfare) state in the development of society. The state stood for the good, and science and rationality were its foremost instruments.

The background to *Kris i befolkningsfrågan* was that the birth-rate in Sweden had been steadily falling since the latter part of the nineteenth century, and was regarded as critical during the 1930s. The state Population Commission began its work in 1935. The social debate was dominated by two issues: the need for more children to be born, and the fact that more children should be born within those groups with a better social position (see, for example, Hatje 1974 and Kälvemark 1980). The Myrdals' work must be viewed against that background. The Myrdals aimed at a transformation cf society which affected both production and reproduction. Social planning would be carried on under rational control. People's happiness would be a product of the rationally planned society.

The Myrdals' reforms comprised several measures, many of which were aimed at strengthening the institution of the family. Measures were included here for marriage as well as for childbirth and the raising of children. Reforms such as housing loans and rent allowances would facilitate forming a family. Other reforms had to do with maternity and child care, school medical care, school meals, and so on. These general reforms would be supplemented by reforms more directed towards poor mothers and children, for example. But these reforms would not be implemented completely unconditionally. In return, people would have to learn the skills of living, eating, dressing and bringing up their children. That the social engineers knew best, could distinguish the good from the bad, and had to act with authority, was both obvious and stood to reason. It is therefore natural that Alva Myrdal (1944) can write:

> '*The most hardened sinners against sound living habits will remain unmoved by such mild influences. They can only be reached through an effective public inspection of dwellings. This must in the final instance rest on legislation and the powers of the police, but in its implementation it should naturally avail itself of counselling and personal persuasion. How a control is exercised determines how it is to be built, and in the same way housing inspection should continuously keep a watch over not only the fact that the dwelling does not fall into disrepair, but also give the individual family advice on how best to use their dwelling. The crucial point in modern housing legislation is whether or not we accept a housing inspection that forbids a certain poor standard dwelling from being lived in, or if we are to have someone who will take action against a family who, through their own negligence, allow their children to live below the approved norms of housing hygiene*' (quoted by Hirdman 1989:124).

In the Myrdals' thinking there were two elements which are also to be found in the thinking of the Saint-Simonists: the guiding role of science and the authority.

> '*[The Myrdals] had the scientific refinement that gave them the authority to formulate the norm-giving "should" for the organisation of private life. Knowing how it ought to be gave them "the white man's burden right" towards those who did not know – or did not want to see – their own best, or above all, their children's best.*

> '*In the Myrdals' thinking there were therefore two links in legitimising state encroachment: one of them was scientific competence. If you had that right on your side, you had the moral right to intervene and to make changes, even if people did not wish this. The other link was the right of gifts: if people received help, they had to give something back in return*' (Hirdman 1989:126).

To sum up, it can be stated that Yvonne Hirdman shows how a specific line in the history of ideas runs from the nineteenth-century Utopians to Swedish political welfare work in the 1930s and 1940s. The Utopian image of the future is dominated by rational planning as a means of achieving social harmony and happiness, thereby curing the ills of society. In all essentials, Hirdman finds in the political welfare work of the 1930s and 1940s those basic principles which Saint-Simon and Saint-Simonism stand for; that is, that society is sick and is to be cured with the aid of science, that the work of change is to be planned and carried out by an élite, that the individual is to be subordinate to the authority (the welfare state), and that the work of change is driven by solidarity with (love of) the underprivileged masses.

Saint-Simonism and the social services

In the previous section I presented the ideas that lay behind the big social reform programmes of the 1930s and 1940s, which formed the framework of the way welfare work and social policy developed during the period in question. They were important and crucial programmes for the work of social change. The next central development phase comprises the work of the Commission of Inquiry into the Social Services (hereafter called SU) and the introduction of a new Social Services Act with effect from 1 January 1982. The Act, together with supplementary legislation, was a codification of SU's perception of the causes of social problems, as well as its considerations on aims and means. In this section, I intend to discuss SU's work.

It is my opinion that the norms, views of society and of man reflected in SU's work on the causes of social problems, as well as their basic appraisal of the aims and means of the social services, can be understood in terms of Saint-Simon's thinking and Saint-Simonism. In SU there is a strong belief in the rational and total planning of society as a means of remedying social problems and of achieving social harmony.

Let us first describe the circumstances surrounding SU's work. The political directives for SU were announced on 8 December 1967. SU worked for several years and comprised several reference groups. The Commission's basic judgements, view of society, view of man/woman, discussions about aims and means were presented in a report establishing principles in 1974 (SOU 1974:39). The proposed Bill and opposing points of view were presented three years later in a final report (SOU 1977:40). The work of the Commission resulted in a new Social Services Act, together with supplementary (compulsory) legislation, which replaced the Social Assistance Act of 1956, the Child Care Act of 1960 and the Temperance Act of 1954.

The background to the setting up of SU was a political desire to modernise, co-ordinate and render more effective the legislation in force within the field of social welfare. In the directives, the Minister was of the opinion that changes in society and lines of development within social welfare made a review of the legislation in force necessary. Legislation had to be adapted to developments in society, as well as to the new methods and increased resources that had become available for care and treatment. Methods of care and treatment, co-ordination of measures taken, and co-operation between the different organs of society ought to be revised. Furthermore, the local and regional organisation of social welfare should be looked into, in order to bring about an efficient and rational organisation. It should also be pointed out that the directives to the Commission stipulated that developments on the international scene, and particularly the efforts of the Nordic countries towards harmonisation, should be taken into consideration.

The inquiry was to be very extensive. Work on the first report – establishing principles – was carried out in several reference groups. The kinds of areas dealt with by these groups throw light on the level of ambition and expectations of the Commission as far as the scope of the inquiry was concerned. The following principal areas were of interest: specification of issues to be targeted in social welfare, aims and means of the various main functions of social welfare, families with pre-school children, children and adolescents of and above school age, misusers of addictive drugs, the economy of social welfare, family counselling activities, and social processes.

I shall later discuss SU's work on the overall aims of the social services, and some of the means indicated for the work of them. But before looking into the aims and means of the social services, it would be advisable to present the opinions of the Commission on the causes of social problems, an area which can be directly linked to Saint-Simonism.

The causes of social problems as seen by the Commission of Inquiry into the Social Services
In the first report establishing principles, a great deal of space is devoted to describing and analysing the social processes which have, for a long period of time, predominated in society. A connection is also made with the socio-political ideas and reforms which predominated on the Swedish socio-political scene in the nineteenth and twentieth centuries. The Commission wanted to show that there is a strong link between social changes and social problems:

> *'In this way the negative features of developments will be accentuated. It is important to stress this. The view of special conditions expressed in what follows should therefore not be considered a complete appraisal of how things developed within the areas treated. The continuous structural change going on in society has led to improvements in general social conditions that were previously not thought possible. Many earlier problems have thus disappeared, others have decreased. But certain problems remain, and new ones, often difficult to solve, have arisen. It is these problems that face social welfare today' (SOU 1974:39:207-208).*

In another section of the report, it was emphasised that social problems were connected with the basic social structure and with general developments in society.

The basic structure of society was regarded as the principal source of social problems. Long-term problem-solving measures through social planning were recommended.

The Commission thus saw the causes of social problems in the structure of society itself, and above all in changes within it. On this point, the views of the Commission coincided with Saint-Simon's basic analysis of the causes of social problems. It was, in other words, not a question of individual failings of a psychological or other nature.

The Commission was naturally aware of the possibility of interpreting social changes in terms of integration (consensus) and conflict. On this point, they chose a middle way, and claimed that there were many reasons that spoke for the social change in Swedish society being seen in terms of both integration and conflict. Their opinion was that these aspects complemented one another.

The overall aims of the social services

The social services have been provided with overall aims in the form of three principles, namely democracy, equality, and solidarity. Security is another important one. These are also guiding principles in other areas of Swedish society. Seen from the perspective of the issues raised in this chapter, it is above all the concept of democracy which is interesting. Let us see what democracy means to the actors within the social services, that is, political representatives, professional social workers, and clients.

It is the politicians who have to make the important decisions concerning the fundamental organisation of social welfare with regard to aims, contents and means at the municipal level. Professional social workers, or social secretaries as SU chose to call them, are those who work nearest to the political representatives. For the social workers, the principle of democracy means that they can, within the framework of legislation and the decisions of representative bodies, influence the content, methods and working forms of social welfare. What, then, does the principle of democracy entail for the client? In principle, the clients shall have knowledge of the laws and regulations that affect their social care situation. In practice, they should, if possible, have access to the details and information on which the social services base their decisions and courses of action.

According to the intentions of the Social Services Act, it is the political representatives who have the formal power to decide the contents and organisation of social welfare. What happens in reality is naturally more complicated, and deviates from the ideals codified by the social services. In reality, politicians and social workers stand for two separate but connected parts of the social services. There is, thus, an alliance between these two groups as regards the management of social welfare, objectively and from the client's perspective (see, for example, Beckman 1985 and Ronnby 1981). Ultimately, the relationship between the parties crystallises, and the political representative and social worker stand against the client/citizen.

The instruments of the social services

The report divides the tasks of the social services into eight main functions:

- participation in the planning of society
- general preventive work
- information
- means-tested financial help
- social services
- support and treatment in open social care
- institutional care and treatment
- social control.

I wrote earlier that there is a strong element of Utopian intention in the report, as well as a belief in the rational and total planning of society as a means of remedying social problems and of achieving social harmony. This belief in rational and total social planning is clearly reflected in the main functions of the social services. Over and above this, more or less explicitly stated, there are a number of features in the main functions of the social services which strongly resemble their inheritance from Saint-Simonism. I am thinking mainly of the structure of society as a principal source of social problems (the sick society), the importance of science to curing social problems, the educational role of society (the welfare state) in bringing up its citizens, social control in a wide sense, and the social services as a model of social change. In what follows, I shall discuss some of the main functions of the social services to illustrate how the inheritance from Saint-Simon is reflected in the thinking of the Commission.

The role of the social services in the planning of society

As I pointed out earlier, SU puts forward the argument that social problems are mainly the result of the basic structure of society and of general developments in society. SU therefore tries to find the long-term and constructive means of combating social problems in the planning of society. What is more precisely meant by the planning of society is not clear from the work of the Commission.

It is, however, evident that they agree with a general view that society is in fact planned in different ways. This can be seen, for example, when SU writes that responsibility for social planning rests on different bodies at national, regional, and municipal levels.

'In this context, the role of social services should be to contribute knowledge to the planning process, to take initiatives, to participate directly in planning, and to activate groups of citizens to take action to influence their situation. The basis for this is to be found in the social services' theoretical knowledge and practical experience of the problems.

Those seeking help represent individual help needs that require support and treatment directed at the individual and their primary group. But they also represent symptoms of the state of society, lack of agreement between the aims of society and social reality, effects of expulsion mechanisms. With its wide contacts with the groups in society that have social problems, the social services at different levels should participate in the compilation of empirical data and causal analyses which can provide a necessary part of the foundation for social planning' (SOU 1974:39:245-246).

This statement contains several characteristic features worth noting to see how the history of ideas tradition with its roots in Saint-Simon's thinking is reflected in SU's line of argument:

a.   The social services are an important control instrument for influencing the structure and general development of society.

b.   The social services shall participate in the planning of society. The social services have 'wide contacts with the groups in society that have social problems'.

c.   The social services have 'theoretical knowledge', they are to compile 'empirical data', and carry out 'causal analyses'. In other words, the social services, with the help of science and rational planning, are to change the structure of society and eliminate social problems.

In connection with the participation of the social services in the planning of society, neighbourhood work and community work are also touched on.

'The term "community work" is usually used as a name of social care methods practised to a large extent in certain other countries. Up to now in Sweden, it has been tried out in some cases under the name of

*"community work". Recently, the name "neighbourhood work" has
begun to be used instead, as this better describes what the methodology
entails, that is treating group or environmental problems in the local surroundings. It may be a question of child upbringing, youth problems,
general leisure problems, and so on. It may also be shortcomings in the
physical environment as regards housing, traffic, playgrounds, and
premises for recreational activities, service...'* (SOU 1974:39:246-247).

It is, furthermore, emphasised that two principles must apply to this type of
activity. The first principle means that neighbourhood work is to be carried on
within the framework of the aims and guidelines stated in legislation and by the
authorities concerned. There are some interesting features of SU's line of
reasoning on neighbourhood work.

In the first place, neighbourhood work can be a question of child upbringing. It
can also be noted that several of the main functions of the social services are
aimed at child upbringing as well as the upbringing of members of society.
Among other things, information activities of the social services are aimed at
communicating values and knowledge which influence behaviour in the
direction desired.

Secondly, neighbourhood work may concern most of social life, both public
and private. As examples, SU mentions child upbringing, youth problems,
leisure problems, housing, traffic, playgrounds, service, and so on.

The third feature is subtler. SU states that neighbourhood work as a method of
social care is to be carried on within the framework of aims and guidelines stated
in legislation and by the social committees. SU thinks that this is necessary in
order to avoid conflicts between the social worker role and the political representative role. The background to these comments on limitations in neighbourhood
work is not particularly difficult to understand. All work of social change affects
the power, preferences, privileges, shortcomings and so on of various interest
groups. This is especially true of work of social change directed both at the
structure and the development of society. According to the Commission, this is a
source of social problems, and there is, in other words, a dilemma built into work
of social change. Its aim is structural changes, but these are to take place within
the framework of the given social structure, without questioning and threatening
this structure. This is a dilemma that is only summarily dealt with by the
Commission. But SU is consistent in taking such a standpoint, since, as I earlier
pointed out, they interpret social changes in terms of integration and conflict.

The Commission thus choose a golden middle way, thereby camouflaging central problems that are built into their line of reasoning.

The social services and social control
One of the principal functions of the social services is social control, according to SU. At the beginning of the chapter on the instruments of the social services, they write that an element of social control is part of all social activities, and that the issue of the exercising of social control by the social services affects social welfare in its entirety.

The concept of 'social control' is well known in sociological literature. The exactness and usefulness of the concept have been thoroughly discussed (see, for example, Allardt 1965, Durkheim 1953, Mead 1934, Parsons 1951, and Ross 1910). The report, however, confines itself to the following statement:

> '*No society can work if people act without consideration for others. Some form of social control is therefore necessary to make teamwork between people possible, and to reduce the incidence of deviations from desired social behaviour.*
>
> '*In small groups, people can feel a spirit of community and work for common goals. This presupposes that certain agreements are made on how co-operation is to be organised, what loyalty the group demands, and so on.Teamwork between different small groups is more complicated, and here the state, the municipalities and larger organisations assume part of the responsibility for seeing to it that things work satisfactorily, mainly by means of laws and other regulations. But much of this teamwork is regulated by the groups themselves, who often seek support in larger organisations with extensive tasks*' (SOU 1974:39:275).

Among other things, it is here implied that it is a question of social control both in primary groups, such as, for example, the family or circle of friends, and social control in secondary groups, that is to say in groups and institutions with a formal structure and formal systems of norms. To be able to show what SU really means by the concept of social control, I would like to reproduce the following long extract from the report establishing principles, in which social control is summarised in three groups:

> '*a) Social control which guards against norm conflicts and behaviour deviations:*

71

- *influencing norms in day-care centres and other institutions, where the aim is acceptance of society's norms and behaviour that does not conflict with these norms;*

- *general social information with the same purpose;*

- *influence through education and information to achieve increased tolerance of behaviour deviations on the part of individuals or groups which do not harm others;*

- *different kinds of social service that indirectly influence values and behaviour;*

- *arranging various kinds of leisure activities;*

- *measures which facilitate the development of positive, informal social control in the living environment, and so on.*

'b) Social control which entails working in voluntary forms on norm conflicts or behaviour deviations:

- *trying to influence gangs, and other measures aimed at activating clients to work on their problems;*

- *different kinds of voluntary support and treatment efforts in open or institutional forms.*

'c) Social control practised with the aim of making treatment possible or to protect the client:

- *separating children from their home environment if required for the child's best interest;*

- *taking people into care to break an acute destructive situation, and to get treatment started.*

'Social control whose aim is mentioned under c) can sometimes make an intervention necessary without the consent of the client – or of the guardian if that should be the case' (SOU 1974:39:277).

It is possible, on the basis of this long extract, to interpret SU's intentions as regards the control functions of the social services. The following aspects are interesting to note:

a. By 'social control' is meant both control of norm systems and behaviour patterns, and control by society or state control – in other words, forced intervention.

b. Control of norm systems and behaviour patterns concerns a large number of areas, which together, and in practice, embrace our whole life.

c.   The spirit of the presentation is that the social authorities know what is right and what is wrong in norm systems and behaviour patterns.
The social services' 'theoretical knowledge', 'empirical data' and 'causal analyses' form the basis of judgements on what is right and what is wrong.

d.   Social control also means forced intervention. In SU's terminology, this is called 'intervention without the consent of the client'.

e.   The view of the control function of the social services is an elucidation of the fact that Swedish social welfare is basically directed towards judicial-administrative social work, and meets its clients with two faces: a helping one and a controlling one.

To sum up, it can be established that the work of the Commission of Inquiry into the Social Services is dominated by a strong belief in rational and total planning as a means of eliminating social problems and of achieving social harmony.

Elements of Saint-Simon and Saint-Simonism are evident, and in some respects almost over-explicit, in the Commission's report.

Discussion

The continuity in the history of ideas manifests itself in a number of aspects: the premise of the structure and development of society being the basis of social problems; the strong belief in the capacity of science and rational planning to cure the ills of society; the total organisation of people's lives; and belief in the role of the authority. A systematic comparison of Saint-Simonism, the welfare work of the 1930s and 1940s, and the work of the Commission of Inquiry in the 1970s can be tabulated as follows:

TABLE 3.1 Saint-Simonism and Swedish welfare work

	Saint-Simonism	Welfare work 1930s and 1940s	Commission of Inquiry
The structure of society is the basis of social problems	Yes	Yes	Yes
Science will cure the ills of society	Yes	Yes	Yes
An organised authority will control	Yes	Yes	No, formally Yes, in reality
People's lives will be totally organised	Yes	Yes	Yes

Besides the discussion previously, this table gives rise to comments about the idea of authority. The Saint-Simonists in particular explained that social progress and the remedying of problems in society were dependent on the organised authority. Here the authority was almost a sacred character and was linked with God. In Saint-Simon himself, the authority was more dependent on scientific knowledge. The welfare work of the 1930s and 1940s, and its manifestation in the work of the Myrdals, is clear on this point: it was necessary to have organised authority. The authority was the beneficent welfare state with its social engineers, who by force of their scientific rationality knew what was good and bad for people and for society.

When we consider the Commission of Inquiry and its product, the Social Services Act, we are confronted with a doubleness. One of the overall aims of the social services is democracy. Among other things, democracy means the realisation of the will of the people, and of independent opinion forming. SU asserts that people's active participation in the decision-making processes which are of consequence to their life situation is extremely important from the viewpoint of democracy. This, together with SU's statement on the clients' opportunities for making themselves heard within the social services, may give the impression that this is the case. In actual fact, it is a question of a system that stipulates what is best and what is bad for the client/citizen (see also *Ideal och verkligheter i svensk socialvård* 1976, Holmberg 1978, Ronnby 1981, and Beckman 1985). It is my conclusion that the idea of authority is also evident in the thinking of the Commission, as well as in the social services (including the so-called compulsory laws).

To sum up, the table shows that there is an interesting line in the history of ideas, running from Saint-Simon, one of the central figures of social science, to social work as a set of ideas.

I noted earlier in this chapter that the tradition the main features of which were formulated by Saint-Simon was later named 'sociology' by August Comte. The same tradition is called 'sociology as agent activity' by Björn Eriksson. While Comte's concept is formulated generally, Eriksson's is more precise and emphasises the interplay of theory and action. Nowadays there are different kinds of sociologies, in which conceptions of the world, interest in different fields of knowledge, theoretical premises, and so on, vary, and in some cases compete with one another. 'Sociology as agent activity' refers to a tradition in which three elements are combined: a theory about society, a programme of action for the work of change, and a group of people who undertake to implement the work of change.

The Saint-Simon tradition forms a self-evident history of ideas background to the subject of sociology. A chapter on Saint-Simon's thinking has an obvious place in handbooks on the classics of sociology. But what about the subject of social work?

The subject of social work does not have this obvious tradition of having its roots in the central social science schools of history of ideas. The line of development in the history of ideas which I called 'from theory to practice' at the beginning of this chapter has been very much neglected by the discipline of social work. As I see it, this is a mistake for a discipline that must make hard efforts to develop its core, investigate its boundaries, its object of study – its identity as a research discipline.

I have tried to show that there is an empirical base on which social work as a scientific discipline can be established in the line of development of the history of ideas in social science. This line is 'from theory to practice' in general, and in the Saint-Simon tradition in particular. The empirical base is also the one for the subject of sociology. But no discipline has a monopoly of traditions and classics in the history of ideas. It is up to the institutional will and scientific capacity of each discipline to investigate its history of ideas roots and establish itself in these.

As far as the subject of social work in relation to Saint-Simon's thinking is concerned, there are at least two good reasons for the discipline of social work having an advantage over other adjacent disciplines. One of them is the basic structure of social work, in which theory and practice are obvious elements.

The other one is the fundamental interest in knowledge shown by social work, which means that theory exists in order to change social reality, that is, to make life better for mankind and to help those in need. I have good grounds for concluding that the subject of social work can, and should, consider Saint-Simon to be one of its classics.

Chapter 4
Mary Richmond's Contribution
to Social Work

*'... her formulations always grew out of the exigencies of practice –
her own, in Baltimore and Philadelphia, and that of others as reported
in records and institutes.'* (Muriel Warren Pumphrey 1956)

Introduction
In this chapter, we continue to investigate one of the fields generated by the
four-fold table in chapter 2. My starting point will be the field characterised by
the variable values *from practice to theory and the causes of social problems
are to be found in the individual*.

It is within this field of characteristics that Mary Richmond's work occupies a
central position. Richmond is not the first practitioner and thinker who can be
identified in this field. Her practical activities and theoretical work were influenced by several persons (see, for example, Richmond 1930, Pumphrey 1956
and Pumphrey 1957). But the practitioner and thinker who first formulated the
scientific frameworks for the work of social change directed towards the individual was Mary Richmond. Her work also paved the way for a central
tradition within social work, and she initiated new concepts and working
methods. Mary Richmond is a central pioneer within the framework of the
tradition of the history of ideas in question. The purpose of this chapter is to
investigate her work as one of the foundations of the history of ideas in social
work.

In this chapter, my main aim is to investigate the following question: in what
way does Mary Richmond's work and contribution to the development of
social work belong to the tendency in the history of ideas formulated in the theoretical frame of reference 'from practice to theory', and to the fact that the
causes of social problems are to be sought in the individual?

Her life history
Mary Richmond was born in 1861. Her parents died of tuberculosis when she
was small, and she was looked after by her maternal grandmother, who lived in
modest financial circumstances in Baltimore. Her relatives were not
favourable disposed to the schools of that time, and compulsory schooling had
not been introduced. This meant that she did not start school until she was 11
years old. Her grandmother helped her to read, and an acquaintance of the
family's had books that she lent. Reading was Mary Richmond's great passion.

She later wrote of her grandmother that it was she who stimulated her to read constantly. It was also her grandmother who encouraged her to discuss the conditions under which her fellow men and women lived (Richmond 1930, edited by J C Colcord).

After finishing her high school studies in 1878, Mary Richmond moved to New York. There she had problems with her lungs, and, moreover, contracted malaria. She moved back to Baltimore where she made a living as a book-keeper.

Her career in social work began in 1889 when she got a temporary job as a treasurer with the Charity Organization Society of Baltimore. It was an insecure job, but Mary Richmond thought of it as a possible opening to a new working life. She proved very capable and carried out her duties with great success. Despite being young, a woman, and lacking formal education, Mary Richmond was elected secretary-general of the organisation after two years. In 1899, she published her first book, *Friendly Visiting among the Poor*, and received greater recognition as a social worker. When she was offered the chance of building up the Philadelphia Society for Organizing Charity, she realised that she had done what she could in Baltimore and moved to Philadelphia, where she worked for the next decade. It was during this period that Richmond started the teaching in which she developed her 'case method'. When the well-known Russell Sage Foundation was established in 1907, it was predictable that Richmond would be appointed director of one of the departments, the Field Department, in New York. A new period of her life began.

During this period, Mary Richmond was constantly occupied by her teaching, her writing, and by national questions to do with social work. A work schedule, probably dating from 1910, makes interesting reading as it reveals her enormous burden, as well as her capacity for working hard. Mary Richmond had divided the working year into elucidate parts, and planned her activities in terms of these units of working time. This is what her schedule was like:

a. Teaching at schools of social studies, 2 units

b. Charity Organization Institute (as director of studies), 1 unit

c. Writing, 1.5 units

d. Daily correspondence, 1 unit

e. Daily personal contacts, 1.5 units

f. Diverse tasks (visiting organisations, for example), 1.5 units.

It is also during this period that she publishes *Social Diagnosis* (1917), the first comprehensive work on the theory and method of social work. In 1921 she was awarded the honorary degree of Master of Arts at Smith College for 'establishing the scientific basis of a new profession'. Mary Richmond died in 1928.

Starting points

Mary Richmond's achievements in social work are a typical example of the 'from practice to theory' tendency in the history of ideas. Richmond, moreover, started from the viewpoint that the causes of poverty and social problems were to be sought in the individual.

Practical work in the forefront

In this section, I shall give some examples of events and standpoints in Richmond's career and development which give us a picture of why she belongs to the tendency in the history of ideas in which the dominant feature is the primacy of practical work. I shall discuss her involvement in the Myrtle Club, her attitude towards the concept, and social practice, of 'friendly visiting', her thoughts on 'charity organisation', and her outlook on the nature of the education of social workers. Finally, I shall also touch upon her opinion that the causes of social problems are to be sought in the individual.

One of Mary Richmond's earliest commitments was as a member, and later chairwoman, of the Myrtle Club. She became a member at the same time as she started her first job in social work. The Myrtle Club was an organisation for young working girls and women, and its aim was to work with the social and professional problems of its members. At the very beginning of her involvement, Richmond wrote an article that she called 'Don't be an Insulator' (1899) in which the members were encouraged to become deeply involved in social problems, and to fight against them. She believed that it paid to get involved, and recounted how the organisation one year previously had stopped one of Baltimore's largest employers from importing new workers who would have had a negative effect on wages.

Women from charity organisations and social clubs had organised a meeting where machine operators who were members of the Myrtle Club presented the problem. Within a week, an action committee representing 5,000 women had been formed. The work of the action committee resulted in the plans for importing new labour being shelved. Richmond considered that the success of the action was not achieved by a small group of factory women who happened to belong to an organisation for young women, but that it could hardly have been possible without their participation.

The Myrtle Club was Richmond's first platform for social involvement. Just one year after writing the article mentioned above, she made a speech in which she advocated the idea of so-called friendly visitors as an important activity in social work.

Mary Richmond had just become secretary-general of the Charity Organization Society of Baltimore in 1890 when she gave the lecture on friendly visitors. Friendly visiting was seen as a way of alleviating the suffering of the poor. Richmond wrote in 1890 of the background to the idea:

> '*Life in these great cities of ours, where the problems of civilization are being worked out before our eyes, is an intensely interesting thing; but those who have given the matter any thought, cannot but see with anxiety the rapidly widening gulf between class and class – the rich growing richer, and the poor poorer. Do not hope to right the evil by material gifts. You are only adding fuel to the fire. But a much simpler thing would do it – a thing so simple that I am afraid you will not believe in it – simple friendliness*' (Richmond 1930:41).

This act of charity would be based entirely on people's compassion. A friendly visitor was a friend working voluntarily. Friendship would be offered as a social programme in which friendliness itself was the main ingredient. There would be no money or alms. In the same publication she wrote:

> '*Another limitation which cannot be too much insisted upon, is the keeping your relations with the less fortunate as natural as possible. It is not natural for us to regard our friends as sources of supplies, and it is not natural for the poor to so regard you. If you are going to be a* **friend**, *fertile in helpful suggestions, sympathetic and kind, you cannot be an almoner too. I heard a Boston friendly visitor say, last spring, that she had never regretted anything so much in all her work as a loan of 2 dollars which she had made to one of her cases, for it took months to re-establish friendly relations with the woman, who was unable to repay it.*' (Emphasis original.)

These quotations illustrate how well inclined, but also how naïve, Mary Richmond was in her hopes of friendly visitors being able to alleviate the suffering of the poor in a society where the rich got richer, and the poor poorer.

Richmond's naïvety was to diminish as she grew in experience and knowledge. In her later works, articles and lectures, as well as books, she developed her views on voluntary social work. Introducing and developing professional social work took a more and more central place in her endeavours. The furtherance of professional social work took place against the will of the friendly visitors. In an article in 1907, Richmond stressed the interplay between professional, paid social workers and voluntary, friendly visitors. She was of the opinion that the charity organisations must help the voluntary visitors by giving them information about the families to be visited, and about the likelihood of the visit being a success. Furthermore, the professional charity organisations should assist by interpreting the experiences of the friendly visitors in connection with the visit, and relate these experiences to existing circumstances. Richmond was careful to emphasise that the charity organisations had no reason to get involved in the lives of those seeking help if they were not entirely certain that this help could be effective. She had the same attitude towards making use of friendly visitors: if they were not sure that their help could be effective and useful, they should not use their services. Richmond was concerned about the nature of co-operation, and wrote:

> 'We hear much about trained paid workers in these days, but the supreme test of a trained worker is the ability to turn to good account the services of the relatively untrained. The better the friendly visitor, the higher the standard of professional charitable service that he will demand, and the higher the standard of professional service, the more good friendly visitors there will be. This is not merely a cheering example of reciprocity; it is the larger half of social reform' (Richmond 1930:260-61).

Richmond was not only involved in the issues brought to the fore by the voluntary friendly visitors. With her appointment as treasurer of the Charity Organization Society of Baltimore, she became closely involved with the issues confronting charity organisations. Her work was practical; she met people, organised the work, dealt with financial matters, and so on. She also documented her work in innumerable lectures and articles. It was to prove later that this documentation would form the starting point of her theoretical works. On the basis of practical social work, she formulated working principles, theoretical approaches and methods.

In connection with finishing her work in Baltimore, she wrote an article, published in 1900, in which she presented her views on the position of the charity organisations at that time (Richmond 1930). The article was systematically structured and comprised the following topics: the objectives of the charity organisation, the organisation's social welfare policy, co-operation with various interested parties, systematic investigation, registration of social welfare measures taken, constructive work, friendly visits, and education and training matters.

Richmond looked on charity as a spiritual force. Insufficient knowledge and imperfect organisation meant that the charity organisations functioned as a blind force; she thought that they made things worse for those seeking help instead of helping. We should strive towards enlightened and well-organised charity activities which could be strong social forces. The spirit of charity is to be found everywhere in the world, in the hearts of many people, but is unable to solve the problems that these well-intentioned people want to solve. Richmond was of the opinion that the charity organisations were incompetent. She wished that it would be possible for positive forces to be an effective instrument for helping the needy.

In the article there are two aspects that should be emphasised in this context. Firstly, Richmond's strong commitment to charity, that is, social work as practical activity. The article bears witness to the fact that she lived in, with and for social work. She stresses its central importance as a social institution. Secondly, Richmond's insight into the fact that charity must be organised in a systematic and professional way. The charity organisation must have a definite aim, an organisational policy. Likewise, attention must be paid to matters of training and education. It is this aspect which forms the background to her interest in theory, which I shall go into in the next section.

In her doctoral dissertation on Mary Richmond, Muriel Warren Pumphrey (1956:160) emphasises Richmond's practical work as the principal source of her knowledge of social work:

> '*It might be interesting to pause to compare the kind of preparation for social work practice Mary Richmond acquired in her first position with the knowledge and skills a social work recruit sixty-five years later has to offer after graduation from a two-year course in a modern school of social work. Her assignments in practice had undoubtedly been more intensive and more varied; she had had more opportunity to try out her own hunches and learn from mistakes. She had had a chance to see the inner workings of an agency as a participant, to watch its policy formation, and to sense the quality of its leadership in a way that careful supervision and the intricate administrative organization of today's big agencies seldom permit a modern student to more than observe from afar. She had had to find out almost entirely on her own initiative what accumulated knowledge and experience could offer to save her from*

unsound methods; much that she read was repetitive, contradictory, or inapplicable; many contributions which might have been helpful never came to her attention.'

Another fact that shows Mary Richmond's opinion of the importance of practice in relation to theory is her view of the education of social workers. In two articles (Richmond 1930) presented in 1897, she discussed her views on the education of social workers and warned against it being too closely connected to the university. Before giving her views on the matter, I think it is important to describe the educational situation of 'charity workers', as social workers were called in the United States at that time, in the second half of the nineteenth century.

The development of social science in the United States was closely associated with studies of social problems and the work of social change. One of the main aims of The American Social Science Association (ASSA) was to promote the application of scientific methods for solving social problems. Many persons involved in studies of social problems at various American universities towards the end of the nineteenth century had been on courses organised by ASSA members at Johns Hopkins University (Broadhurst 1971).

'Philosophy II' was the name of a course developed as early as 1885 by Francis G Peabody, a well-known professor at Harvard University. The course was very similar to those on sociology given at other universities such as Yale, Columbia, and Smith College. Many of the students on these courses later became leading figures in the field of social work. The course comprised the following items: ethical questions in social reform programmes; questions concerning charity, divorce, the Indian population, work, prisons and temperance; lectures, essays and practical observation. It is interesting to note that when Professor Peabody was to hold the course for the first time, it was questioned whether it could be included in the ordinary university programme. The course seemed all too unconventional in the academic world. The university authorities only accepted the course because of the prestige enjoyed by Peabody within the academic world (Bruno 1948). Some years later, they started giving even more advanced courses at other universities, especially at the departments of sociology. At the end of the nineteenth century, the relationship between sociology and social work was a central topic of discussion. Many people thought that the two subjects had their own specific fields of work: sociology should chart general laws and principles that govern human interaction; social work should provide data, try out principles, and carry out practical social work. Frank J Bruno, who wrote a history book on the evolution of social work in the United States, characterised the relationship between theory and practice during this period as 'the honeymoon stage', in other words it was a relaxed period for sociology and practical social work. It was a general conception that studies in sociology were the best way of preparing for social work. It was this tendency that Mary Richmond was against.

Richmond put forward her opinions in the two articles from 1897. She was to maintain this attitude for her entire professional life. The core of her thinking was that social work as the 'art of helping' was a practical activity and, as such, was not dependent on just a single science but on many. She put forward a case against the integration of the education of social workers in the university so that it could develop its own distinctive character as a practical activity. Richmond proposed that a new school for the education of social workers should be called 'The Training School in Applied Philanthropy'. Her ideas had their beginnings in a lecture held in 1893 by another social worker, Anna Dawes. Dawes was the first to propose a special education for the profession of social worker. She claimed that it was important that experienced social workers taught, and shared their experience with, future social workers. According to Dawes, this would make it easier for new social workers to take over from those retiring from the profession without having to repeat mistakes. She also thought that this system of education ensured more security for the clients. It is important to remember that Dawes presented her ideas at the International Congress of Charities and Correction at a time when trained social workers received their education on university courses of sociology, philosophy, and other subjects.

Mary Richmond took note of Dawes's ideas and, in her articles from 1897, outlined a plan of how such a course of education should be designed and organised. She was careful to stress that the curriculum should give priority to practical work instead of academic knowledge. The school should maintain close co-operation with institutions and organisations which offered social work, or charity as it was then called. Classroom teaching should run parallel with practical teaching in the field. As regards choosing the head of the school, she wrote that what they needed was 'a university-trained man who is now engaged in charity work, and who has had wide, practical experience in it' (Richmond 1930).

She also expressed this attitude in her relations with other professionals. Jessie Taft, who had just been awarded her doctorate, went to see Mary Richmond, then at the Russell Foundation, to hear whether she could get a job in social work. Taft's academic qualification did not impress Richmond very much, and she recommended her to practise first at a casework office under a competent supervisor, for example Johanna Colcord (Robinson 1962). Eventually Jessie Taft became a famous social worker and trainer of social workers.

In summary, it can be established that one of the foundations of Mary Richmond's development in social work is the fact that she has her roots in practical social work. Practical social work is, for Richmond, primary, and this is reflected in her practical activities and in her thinking. The principal manifestation of this is her lifelong commitment to practical social work. In addition, she is convinced that it is possible to change social reality, that is, have some effect on poverty and the poor. She has also a clear idea of charity (social work being an almost spiritual force) and that the people seeking help are in need of a friend. Furthermore, it is also important to point out that in her daily practical work, there are the beginnings of elements of systematising and organising, and a strong feeling for knowledge and education – necessary ingredients in putting social work on a theoretical and scientific basis.

Seeking the causes of social problems in the individual
In my theoretical frame of reference, in which the interplay of theory and practice on the one hand and attitude towards the nature of the causes of social problems on the other are discussed, Mary Richmond illustrates the line which signifies that the causes of social problems are to be sought in the individual.

Mary Richmond's attitude, or basic assumption, can best be seen in her controversy with Jane Addams. Addams considered that the causes of social problems should be sought in society. Richmond's model and casework method are based on the standpoint that the causes of social problems are to be sought in the individual. She was, however, not unaware of the influence society had when it comes to social problems; in this connection she used the concept of 'mass betterment'.

Mary Richmond and Jane Addams were two contemporaneous personalities who influenced the practice and theory of social work in opposition to each other. The central issue that divided them was which methods were to be used to have any effect on poverty and social problems. This question must be immediately linked to the question of causes of social problems; you could develop different types of theories and methods depending on which assumptions you made, or which diagnosis you arrived at. Carel Germain and Ann Hartman (1980), commenting on this controversy, are of the very definite opinion that the charity organisations considered the poor to be responsible for their own poverty. Many adherents of charity, especially Mary Richmond, were not interested in structural changes.

Mary Richmond had at an early stage adopted the opinion that the causes of social problems were in individuals themselves. If you had a social problem, you were responsible for it yourself. Several people had influenced her in this direction, the two most important being John Glenn and Josephine Shaw Lowell. More about Glenn and Lowell can be found in Pumphrey 1956 and Leiby 1978. Glenn was a lawyer and chairman of the charity organisation's working committee in Baltimore. He had very long experience of charity work and was in his 70s when Richmond came to Baltimore. Lowell was a social worker and a prominent figure in the world of charity work. She had written quite a lot, and Richmond had read her writings at an early stage of her career. But there were also other people who influenced Richmond in the same direction. There were both extremists and sensible people in the circles that discussed philosophical assumptions on the nature of poverty and the 'guilt' of individuals in this context. One such extremist was Cardinal Gibbons, Bishop of Baltimore, who made the following statement in his address at the 1890 National Conference of Charities and Corrections:

'No matter what efforts may be made by philanthropists and social econ-
omists for the removal of poverty, we must make up our minds that
poverty, in one shape or another, will always exist among us. The words
of Christ will ever be verified, "The poor ye always have with you". It is
in accordance with the economy of Divine Providence that men should
exist in unequal conditions in society – for the exercise of benevolent
virtues' (Pumphrey 1956:179).

Another person who stood close to Richmond, Doctor Weld, did not accept Gibbons's statement because, as well as 'The poor ye always have with you', you could also quote 'There shall be no more poor' (Pumphrey ibid). Weld regarded poverty as a moral problem. Richmond was not an adherent of extreme ideas, but she was convinced that 'individuals were wholly responsible for their own circumstances' (Pumphrey ibid).

Mary Richmond's greatness as far as social work is concerned lies very much in her early contributions to the theory and method of the subject. In *Social Diagnosis* (1917) and *What is Social Case Work?* (1922), she developed a theoretical model and a working method which were to leave a deep mark on social work from then on. The ideas developed in these books are founded on the basic assumption that the causes of social problems should mainly be sought in the individual. The casework method puts the focus on the individual.

Despite her polemics against those who sought the causes of social problems in society, and in particular against Jane Addams, and despite the basic premise on which casework rested, Mary Richmond was not unaware of the fact that the causes of social problems could also be sought in society. She began her great pioneering book, Social Diagnosis (1917:25), with the following insight:

> *'The social workers of the United States form a large occupational group. A majority of them are engaged in case work – in work, that is, which has for its immediate aim the betterment of individuals or families, one by one, as distinguished from their betterment in the mass. Mass betterment and individual betterment are interdependent, however, social reform and social case work of necessity progressing together.'*

Richmond came back to the same standpoint in her later book *What is Social Case Work?* Even if she herself concentrated on social problems at the individual level, and partly at the group level, she was aware of the broad spectrum of approaches to problems and measures that could be taken in social work. In her many lectures she used a diagram, 'The rhythm of social work' (Richmond 1930), which illustrates her view of the development of social work in terms of the work of change in both the individual and in society. As the diagram is little known I reproduce it overleaf

The diagram is somewhat difficult to interpret, and there are none of the texts of the lectures that accompanied it either. Richmond (1930:584), however, commented on the diagram on a couple of occasions in the following way:

> *'An interesting characteristic of a spiral is the fact that though it returns again and again to the same general position, the return is . . . higher up. For the last fifty years, the swing of the spiral has been between mass betterment on the one hand and individual betterment on the other.*
>
> *When social movements, social agencies, social workers, have a conception of development and advance which **includes** both the welfare of the individual and of the mass, which reconciles these two points of view and assures the permeation of each by each, then the upward climbing spiral to which I referred in the beginning will no longer lose its balance and momentum by swinging violently from one side to the other. It will take a far wider, firmer sweep in both directions, it will cover more ground more symmetrically. In some such way as this, as I see it, social work will at last come into full possession of itself and of its rightful field of service.'* (Emphasis original.)

FIGURE 4.1 The development of social work
Source: Richmond 1930: 589

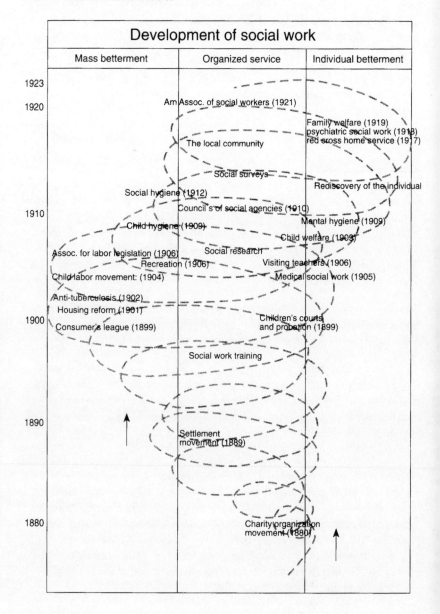

To sum up, it can be said that in both her theory and method books Mary Richmond's starting point was that the causes of social problems should mainly be sought in the individual. However, she acknowledged the fact that the work of social change was carried out and should also take place in relationship to society ('mass betterment'), which means that the causes of social problems could also be sought in society, an opinion which she successfully opposed in her duels with Jane Addams. Richmond's acknowledgement of the importance of work of structural social change is also apparent when she defines four forms of social work: social casework, group work, social reformism, and social research. But she is once again inconsistent when she discusses what type of data should be collected for social diagnosis. To the eternal question of 'Shall we change the individual or the surroundings?' she develops a conciliatory position. Seen from our modern point of view, and especially from the Scandinavian perspective, she definitely chooses the individual. The development of the client's personality is at the core of her thinking. In both practical social work and in her later theoretical works, she was mainly oriented towards the individual, and it was the individual who was to be cured.

Links to theory
If the first part of Mary Richmond's professional life is characterised by practical social work, the second half is by her efforts to establish theoretical insights and theories on the base of her practical experience. This period of Richmond's activities moves around two concepts, 'social diagnosis' and 'social casework'. These concepts were also the titles of her two most important books, which were published in 1917 and 1922. In *Social Diagnosis*, she develops all the details of her social casework method, while in *What is Social Case Work?* she discusses and develops the theoretical framework for her method. While the first book is in a large format and contains about 500 large pages, the second comprises only about 250 pages of smaller format.

The social casework concept may have been originated by Edward T. Devine, one of the earlier secretaries of the charity organisation in New York. He used the concept in an article in 1897, where he wrote 'good case work involves much thankless labor' (Bruno 1948). A few years later, Mary Richmond wrote some articles in which she described methods that could be used within the framework of social casework, but did not mention the concept as such. In about 1911 the concept was used by several prominent persons in social work. Since that time, the concept has become well established, principally due to Richmond's works, and has influenced generations of social workers.

Richmond's employment with, and involvement in, Baltimore's charity organisation, which had close connections with Johns Hopkins University through the fact that the chairman of the university board was also the chairman of the charity organisation, gave her the opportunity of coming into contact with scientific thinking. At Johns Hopkins there was a medical school, and many medical students worked as friendly visitors (Becker 1964 and Broadhurst 1971). The influence of scientific medical thinking is evident in Richmond. In *Social Diagnosis* she points out at the beginning how social workers and doctors had worked together to improve the public health situation in New York. Even if various specialities had influenced her social diagnosis, the most marked influence was that of the socio-medical field. Work in social medicine had been started in the United States by Dr Richard C Cabot at the Massachusetts General Hospital in 1905. In the social worker Dr Cabot had seen the potential for complementary and better treatment. It was Dr Cabot's ambition to integrate medical and social work.

In *Social Diagnosis* Richmond develops what is, in effect, a scientific manual of methods. The underlying perspective is borrowed from the natural sciences and can be described as positivist. The process leading to social diagnosis, and thereby to the drawing up of a plan of treatment for the client, consists of various parts: (1) collection of evidence about the client; (2) collection of evidence about the client's family; (3) collection of evidence about relevant circumstances outside the family. The collection of evidence phase/phases is followed by (4) a comparison of evidence from different sources ('inference'); (5) interpretation of evidence, that is, relating the evidence to a given theoretical context ('interpreting its meaning'). The concept of social casework comes into the picture to emphasise the fact that each single client should be treated as a case. Each case follows the process described.

The terminology used by Richmond in this book from 1917, among others, is still used in modern positivist-oriented social science methodology books (see, for example, Blalock 1961, Yin 1984). It was, naturally, not Mary Richmond's intention to write a manual of general scientific methods for the social sciences, which it is important to bear in mind when drawing parallels between *Social Diagnosis* and modern social science methodology books. Her intention was to write a manual of methods for a scientific assessment of *client work in social work* in general and *social casework* in particular. It is also important in this context to note that social casework was not the same thing as social work in general. As Mary Richmond saw it, casework was one type of social work.

Let me here give some examples of Richmond's terminology and descriptions as an illustration of her brilliant contributions to scientific assessment in client work. Richmond (1917:55-56) devotes two chapters to the concept of social evidence and tries to qualify the concept in relation to other concepts. She writes, for example:

> '*The words evidence and proof are often confused.* **Evidence** *is the ultimate fact or facts offered as a basis for inference;* **inference***, a part of the process of reasoning from this fact or facts to another – unknown – fact; while proof is the result of the reasoning. In social diagnosis, the kind of evidence available, being largely testimonial in character, can of course never show a probative value equal to that of facts in the exact sciences. All that is possible for us is to obtain proof that amounts to a reasonable certainty. Social treatment is even more lacking in precision than the treatment of disease . . . This is true partly because social work has as yet amassed but a small body of experience, partly because its treatment demands for success an understanding of "characterology", for which no satisfactory body of data yet exists, but most of all because, for the social case worker, the facts having a possible bearing upon diagnosis and treatment are so numerous that he can never be sure that some fact which he has failed to get would not alter the whole face of a situation.*' (Emphasis original.)

In addition, Richmond avails herself of legal tradition and differs between various types of 'evidence' or social facts: 'real evidence' is facts as we understand them; 'testimonial evidence' is our convictions; 'circumstantial evidence' is indirect convictions that lead to facts which we are interested in. Other distinctions such as 'oral testimony', 'documentary evidence', 'expert evidence', and 'character evidence' are also taken up, and in this connection the importance of the *reliability* of social facts is dealt with. Social facts are to be interpreted and used for the purpose of drawing conclusions. Inference' is the process by which you can derive conclusions about unknown conditions from known facts. Richmond thinks that you can derive a general truth from several particular cases, and that you can derive new facts about a particular case from a general truth. Without calling them by name, she discusses induction and deduction in the assessment of client cases. The first step in the deduction process is to set up hypotheses, which must be tested, she says. Access to data and perseverance in the testing of hypotheses are important factors for success in casework.

The first chapter of the book is focused on issues of the philosophy of science, even if the issues are sparingly substantiated. The interplay between the collection of data and analysis is discussed in a simple, uncomplicated way. Seen from the knowledge we have today and our awareness of scientific-theoretical problems, Richmond's presentation seems rather naïve. Seen from how far social work had advanced in her day, Richmond is a breaker of new ground. It can also be seen from the quotation above that she is aware of the complexity of social life, and of the limitations of positivist methodology in a way that was expressed by Max Weber (1949).

The other parts of Richmond's book are made up of a detailed examination of a number of data collection and documentation techniques, with special reference to the sources of data and the client's relationships that would be relevant to planning future treatment and change.

In her book *What is Social Case Work?* (1922), Mary Richmond discusses basic assumptions and theoretical starting points for social casework. She writes: 'The purpose of this small book is . . . to inquire into *what* social casework is and why it is.' In this sense, the book is a development of the working method she presented in *Social Diagnosis* and the establishing of a theoretical base for the method. The central idea of the book is given the following definition: 'social casework consists of those processes which develop personality through adjustment consciously effected, individual by individual, between men and their social environment'.

As the definition states, the interplay between the individual and their social environment is emphasised. It is this feature that is specific to social casework, Richmond says. She regards casework as its own field of activity, separate from more individually oriented activities carried on in areas such as psychiatry, psychology, and medicine. On this subject she writes (1922:98):

> *'That field is the development of personality through the conscious and comprehensive adjustment of social relationships, and within that field the worker is no more occupied with abnormalities in the individual than in the environment, is no more able to neglect the one than the other. The distinctive approach of the case worker, in fact, is back to the individual by way of his social environment, and wherever adjustment must be effected in this manner, individual by individual, instead of in the mass, there some form of social case work is and will continue to be needed. So long as human beings are human and their environment is the world, it is difficult to imagine a state of affairs in which both they and the world they live in will be in no need of these adjustments and readjustments of a detailed sort.'*

Richmond says that social casework is based on insights and acts. The insights are, on the one hand, insights into the individual and their specific qualities and, on the other, into the resources, dangers and influences of the social environment in relation to the individual. The most important thing is the insight into the inter-action between the individual and their social environment. Regarding acts, she distinguishes between direct and indirect acts/treatment methods. The direct method is the social worker's direct influence on the client through dialogue and advice. This method presupposes a trusting relationship between the social worker and the client. Here a knowledge of psychology is important, says Richmond. The indirect method is the changing of the client's social environment. An understanding of social conditions, and therefore a knowledge of sociology, is important.

Richmond (1922) builds her line of argument on three basic assumptions about human beings.

Firstly, people are *mutually dependent*. This assumption is also one about the relationship between man and society. People's mutual dependence is of central importance to Richmond, and in it she almost sees a spiritual force. When discussing people's mutual dependence, she takes the same view as Durkheim on the relationship between man and society: good social order promotes good personality in the members of society. The art of social casework will in this connection be the art of discovering and ensuring the best possible social relationship with the individual.

Secondly, people are *different*. This assumption leads to the fact that social casework must treat people on the basis of their individual qualities and living conditions. A genuinely democratic social programme creates equal opportunities for all through general measures, at the same time as it also develops an administrative organisation which can tailor-make individual treatment programmes as the individual shows special characteristics.

Thirdly, people are *active beings*. They have their own wills and their own aims in life. In a social casework situation, therefore, the individual can work together with the social worker and influence their own situation.

Mary Richmond says that the book on theoretical issues of the casework model is based on her personal experience and on her reading of many social cases. Typically enough, she begins her book with detailed descriptions of six cases, each of which can illustrate social situations with different elements. She derives her two key concepts, insights and acts, from systematised descriptions of these cases; the characteristic features that she reads in social reality generate her theoretical concepts.

The ideas presented by Richmond in her two books *Social Diagnosis* and *What is Social Case Work?* form a whole, and also reflect her long professional life as a social worker. Richmond's work can best be understood by means of a dialectical model of theory of knowledge (Liedman 1973). The model of 'the dialectical path of knowledge' aims to show the interaction between theory and living context. According to the model, each phenomenon is part of a whole, that is, a universal context. The components in this context must be theoretically processed in order that one may gain a deeper understanding of the whole.

Two pairs of concepts are used in the model: *concrete and abstract,* and *theory and practice*. Liedman says that there must be a co-ordination between these concepts; practice must be on the concrete plane, that is in the living diversity of life. The equivalent of practice on the intellectual plane is the concrete analysis in which the whole range of circumstances is taken into account. In order for the concrete to be applicable to practice, an abstraction (theorising) must take place. This means that certain components that are more crucial than others are selected from the immediate diversity of the whole. In principle, such a process of abstraction eventually provides a universally applicable theory. The next step in the model consists in a movement towards the concrete. The abstract ideas, the theory, must move to the concrete level, to practice, where the theory can be used for concrete analysis and action.

The 'dialectical path of knowledge' model, applied to a description of Richmond's achievements, and as an example of the 'from practice to theory' tendency in the history of ideas, can be illustrated by the following figure:

FIGURE 4.2 The dialectical path of knowledge

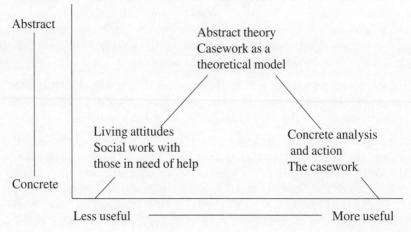

As can be seen from the figure, Richmond's work begins on the concrete plane: she works as a social worker, administers social work, is involved in the service of the needy. Her long and concrete experience in social work, and her thoughts around it, shows the way to a process of abstraction that results in two important books in which Richmond develops a theoretical model for social casework as one type of social work. The model also comprises rules (method) for the concrete work of change (action) in social work. Richmond's theoretical model is not a model at a high level of abstraction. It is, however, theorising that raises her experience to an abstract level by the fact that experience and systematic observation of practical social work are structured, typologised and become universally applicable in a way that they were not previously.

Summary

In this chapter, I have discussed Mary Richmond's work as one of the foundations of the roots of the history of ideas in social work. The empirical investigation is governed by the theoretical frame of reference I presented in chapter 2. This frame of reference generates four fields of characteristics, each of them representing traditions in the history of ideas in the evolution of social work as a practical activity and as a research discipline. I have investigated Mary Richmond's work from the perspective of one of these fields. The tradition in the history of ideas in question is characterised by social work developing within the framework of the 'from practice to theory' tendency, that the causes of social problems are to be sought in the individual, and that treatment should therefore be concentrated on the individual in order to remedy social problems. I have asserted that Mary Richmond is the foremost classic in this connection.

I have shown that there is, in Richmond's work, a distinct element that signifies that developments in social work start with practical social work and then generate a theoretical base. Mary Richmond's early activities are characterised by a marked practical orientation, comprising various forms of social work. I have given several examples of her practical work. On this practical foundation she then built a theoretical construction, with the concepts of social diagnosis and social casework as central elements. On the basis of a line of reasoning developed by Sven-Erik Liedman, I characterised this interplay between practice and theory in Richmond as 'the dialectical path of knowledge'. I have also shown Richmond's primary interest in the individual, in whom she sought the causes of social problems. Consequently, in developing her principal instrument for the work of social change, the social casework method, it was natural for her to direct her efforts towards the social problems diagnosed in the individual.

Mary Richmond's achievements were epoch-making in the field of social work. She coined the term 'social casework', a concept that was to be further developed in various ways. She never used the term 'psychosocial work', and neither was social casework as a concept intended to be psychosocial work such as that into which it has developed today. But it can be claimed without any doubt that Mary Richmond's work and the tradition that developed after her, when seen from a history-of-ideas perspective, form a background to modern psychosocial work. These later developments are also illustrative of the relationship between social work and psychology, a theme that will be discussed in the next chapter.

Chapter 5
Influences from Psychology

Introduction

One of the areas of characteristics in our four-field table (Chapter 2) is generated by the fact that the tendency in the history of ideas runs from theory to practice and that the causes of social problems are to be sought in the individual. 'From theory to practice' means that theoretical knowledge and research results form the basis of social practice, the work of social change. This field also means that the individual is perceived as the source of social problems. As we saw in Chapter 2, in certain circles in the nineteenth century, the individual was considered sick, and they thought that psychopathological and moral defects in the individual created social problems. As progress was made in scientific thinking, there was a growing realisation that psychological or psychiatric factors as well as sociological factors, like inadequate norm learning and norm adaptation, were the mechanisms that created social problems. To get rid of social problems, these mechanisms should be attacked. The field of ideas in question forms the basis for thinkers who considered that individuals possessing these mechanisms in their turn generated social problems.

It is mainly psychology and psychiatry that interact with social work in this field of ideas. Seen from the perspective of a history of ideas, there is a clear connection between developments in this field of ideas and the field discussed in the previous chapter. There, Mary Richmond's work was presented as a prime example of the development of the field of knowledge characterised by the 'from practice to theory' tendency in the history of ideas, and by the individual being the source of social problems. As we saw earlier, there is a distinct element in Richmond's work which means that progress in social work begins with practical social work followed by the development of a theoretical foundation. Richmond mainly sought the causes of social problems in the individual. She developed the concept of social casework as the principal idea in the work of social change.

Social work is influenced by psychology and psychiatry both before and after the breakthrough of the concepts of social diagnosis and social casework. The purpose of this chapter is to describe briefly some of these influences. Within this field of knowledge, there is no obvious thinker of decisive importance to the development of social work as a scientific discipline, and the chapter therefore limits itself to describing the general relationship between psychological approaches, and social work in the form of psychosocial work.

In the evolution of the history of ideas in the social sciences, there is a marked dynamic between the 'from practice to theory' and 'from theory to practice' tendencies. This is true both of the idea that social problems are generated by society and that social problems are generated by individuals themselves. We have already seen that Mary Richmond's practical work of social change resulted in the development of a theory for social work in general and social casework in particular. The development of social casework runs parallel with the attempts of psychology to tackle social problems, when the two sides were both in agreement and disagreement with each other. Even at an early stage of the discipline's development, there is a field of tension between social work and psychology.

Early approaches

Social work with individuals and families has its origin in the work of the charity organisations in the United States at the end of the nineteenth century. The terms 'social diagnosis' and 'social casework' were coined during the 1910s and 1920s with the work of Mary Richmond.

The background to the interest of psychology in, and its contributions to, the development of social work is the work done by the state and various organisations to improve social conditions in America. The first marked contribution can be found in the convening of a national conference on child health care in 1910. The purpose of the conference was to gather scientists, practitioners and administrators to discuss the organisation of child health care in America. The chairman of the conference was the psychologist G Stanley Hall, who had studied children's development, activities and interests since 1883 by means of surveys. Hall and others formed a so-called child study movement. The involvement of psychology in the field of social work was reinforced by two other development trends, namely the recognition of the importance of the sexual drive to behaviour and the development of psychological test methods for studies of individual differences.

A number of works were published within the field around the turn of the century. Many institutions founded research centres for child health care and studies of children's development, and at the same time interest in studies of criminal and mentally retarded children and adolescents increased. Social workers were very interested in studying and using the knowledge gained in psychology. The psychologist William Healy attempted to integrate insights and knowledge from psychology, psychiatry and sociology to reinforce social work. In his book *The Individual Delinquent* (1915), Healy reported studies that he ran at the Juvenile Psychopathic Institute in Chicago, of which he was director. In a lecture given to the national conference of social workers in 1917, he said: 'From psychology the social worker can learn about different types of weaknesses and peculiarities in the individual which are defined as conceptual entities. I want to emphasise that knowledge of how these entities affect the individual's psyche, and what the social consequences of this are, must be a basic working tool for social workers' (quoted by Robinson 1930:27).

Psychiatry also began to influence social work during the 1910s. Dr Adolf Meyer of Phipps psychiatric clinic at Johns Hopkins University, and Dr August Hoch, regarded as prominent figures in modern psychiatry in the United States, contributed to the development of social work through their studies of mental disorders and techniques for handling them. The most definite indication of the importance of psychiatry to social work was made in 1909 with the creation of The National Committee for Mental Hygiene. This organisation aimed to prevent 'insanity' by control of alcohol abuse and venereal diseases at the same time as it modernised views on mental illnesses. Social workers were influenced by the work of the organisation and took in the new insights.

Mary Richmond's books *Social Diagnosis* and *What is Social Case Work?* provided a collected theoretical and methodological basis for social work, and became basic reading in social work in general and casework in particular. In the decades following their publication, a lively working process took place which contributed to the development of the casework method in various ways. This process can be characterised as the attempts of psychology and social work to solve what were considered to be social problems in the individual and, to a certain extent, in the family.

After Mary Richmond

Virginia Robinson states in her doctoral thesis *A Changing Psychology in Social Case Work* (1930) that the decades after Mary Richmond were characterised by social work being influenced by various types of psychological and psychiatric approaches. The schools of social work integrated various psychological ideas into their courses. Richmond's attempts to seek an overall picture of social problems in which not only individual but also social elements are present, disappeared as psychological theories became accepted by those representing social work. The so-called 'new psychology', which was used, for example, in connection with foster children, was divided into five categories by Healy: the behaviourist school, Thomas's model, the Adlerian school, the Freudian school, and the Jungian school. Thus several research centres, using different psychological approaches to the development of social work, were set up.

The so-called diagnostic school developed at Smith College, New York School of Social Work (Columbia University) and at the Chicago School of Social Work.

In order to be able to make the correct diagnosis and differentiate treatment according to the client's condition and needs, facts had to be gathered about the client's situation. The diagnostic school was strongly influenced by Freud's theories. As they worked with psychoanalytical models, it was important to pay special attention to the client's early childhood. The focus was on the client's personality, while an assessment of the client's situation was neglected. The relationship between social worker and client was dominated by an authoritarian attitude. The diagnostic school regarded the client's problems as an illness to be treated by the social worker (Bernler and Johnsson 1988).

Another school, called functional, also developed from the 1920s, mainly at the Pennsylvania School of Social Work (Smalley 1970). The leading researcher was Jessie Taft, who had a doctorate in psychology. This school based their thinking on the theories of Otto Rank, the Austrian psychoanalyst. The individual's birth as a trauma with consequences for the personality, the will of the individual to change, the importance of the here-and-now situation, and the importance of the social worker – client relationship were the main elements introduced in social casework. In the treatment situation, it was the clients' desire to change their situation and their ability to receive help that were emphasised. This school was not interested in the client's earlier childhood experiences.

Virginia Robinson examines social work in general and social casework in particular in the light of the influence of psychology. She also develops a theoretical frame of reference for the functional view of social casework. Robinson stresses the relationship between the social worker and the client as the central instrument in the helping process. She makes the basic assumption that the clients know themselves and their situation best, and therefore it is the client who must make change possible. Social workers are given the role of helpers – persons who stand on the client's side and help the client with their professional knowledge and experience. Robinson is therefore in favour of a democratic relationship between social worker and client. Her fundamental attitude can be compared with a similar basic approach in the Swedish Social Services Act (see chapter 3).

The psychosocial school
Mary Richmond's work and the tradition developed after her constitute a history-of ideas background to modern psychosocial work. Some decades after Richmond's work, both psychology and psychiatry played an extensive role in, and had considerable influence on, social work. Psychology and psychiatry made great progress in the investigation of the individual's mental problems.

The prestige and influence enjoyed by these disciplines at European and American universities were beyond dispute. In addition, it was considered 'finer' to work with an individual's intrapsychic problems than to work with their total life situation, which comprises not only mental but social aspects too. Richmond's work was an attempt to study the individual's whole situation, even if it was half-hearted and with a preference for the individual rather than sur-rounding social factors.

Gunnar Bernler and Lisbeth Johnsson, who in their book *Teori för psyko-socialt arbete* (1988) outlined a background to modern psychosocial work, consider that the psychosocial approach grew from the work done by one of the theorists of the diagnostic school, Gordon Hamilton. Hamilton's work also involves an attempt to create a distinctive image for the psychosocial view in relation to psychology. Hamilton was influenced by gestalt psychology and oriented his work towards the whole person. He was interested in the client-in-situation. According to him, the person, the situation, and the interplay between the person and the situation constitute a whole which can only be seen from a psychosocial perspective.

During the 1930s and 1940s, many attempts were made to develop the social casework method. Bertha Reynolds and Charlotte Towle were two theorists who contributed to the debate with several written works. Both of them reacted strongly to the dominance of psychiatry in certain groups of researchers and in social worker circles. They stressed the interaction between the social environ-ment and the individual when it came to social problems. The researcher who was to use the concept of psychosocial work more explicitly was Florence Hollis. She published *Case Work: A Psychosocial Therapy* in 1964; a revised edition was published together with Woods in 1981. In the whole of her work, Hollis strove to give a distinctive profile to psychosocial work, or 'psychosocial therapy' as she termed it, in relation to psychotherapy, and considered these two forms of therapy to be quite distinct activities. She integrated systems theory into the social casework model, and devoted special attention to the client - social worker relationship. The social worker must respect the client; the client's needs must be the starting point for psychosocial work; an understanding of the client must be based on scientific knowledge; the social worker must respect the right of clients to make their own decisions and, if necessary, the social worker must be responsible for the client (Hollis 1970).

After their survey of the roots of psychosocial work, Bernler and Johnsson (1988:27) made the following assessment:

In our historical survey we have chosen to reflect developments in the United States, but new theories have also been put forward in Europe, especially in England. It is, nevertheless, in the USA that the development of the psychosocial approach in casework has taken place. It is regrettable that it took so long for this approach to make an impact in the United States. The influence of psychoanalysis on casework and the often heated conflicts between the diagnostic school and the functional school were factors that hindered progress. The pendulum often swung to one side or the other: either they strongly over-emphasised the intrapsychic factors or the social factors.

'Even if the two schools have inspired each other, no real attempts have been made to integrate the theoretical foundations on which they stand. A combination of Hamilton's holistic view and Hollis's systems thinking with the emphasis placed on structural and processual aspects by the functional school could have been productive to the development of psychosocial treatment work.

'Neither have they succeeded in combining inner and outer changes into a conceptual whole.'

In recent years, Sweden has been the scene of several attempts to illustrate psychosocial work (Egidius 1978; Hessle 1982; Lennéer-Axelson and Thylefors 1982; and Bernler and Johnsson 1985, 1988, 1989). Perhaps the most interesting of these is the work of Bernler and Johnsson in which systems theory and psychodynamic theory are integrated to be adapted to work of social change.

Conclusion

Two of the fields of characteristics in our four-fold table (Chapter 2) are dealt with in Chapter 3 and in this chapter. The fields are intended to describe practical and theoretical approaches relevant to the evolution of the history of ideas in social work. The similarity between these fields of characteristics is that the source of social problems is to be sought in individuals themselves. As I have pointed out earlier, this way of looking at things is to be understood in terms of ideal types. The two fields differ in the matter of which tendency in the history of ideas it is a question of. In the one case, it is a question of a tendency that starts in practice and develops towards theory, while in the other we start at a theoretical level and then develop problem-solving models that are applicable in practice.

From a general point of view, we can see that these two tendencies in the evolution of ideas are in a state of tension with each other. This depends on the fact that social work, through the casework tradition and later through psycho-social treatment work, and psychology, through its battery of theories, have been oriented towards solving social problems at the individual and family levels. The field of tension comprises both co-operation and disagreement between social work and psychology.

There are two main reasons for these two disciplines co-operating with each other. The first one is that social work needs the battery of theories and methods that psychology can provide. By force of its foundation of theories and methods, psychology has a bank of knowledge that is of importance to social work. At different periods of time, social work has tried to find answers in psychological theories in order to develop problem-solving methods.

The other reason is linked to the involvement of psychology in treatment work at the individual level. Psychology is a science of the individual's intrapsychic and interpsychic condition. The discipline also works with conditions regarded as being problematic, and in this context it is natural for psychology to analyse social problems at the individual level and try to develop problem-solving methods. In this way, psychology is working in the same area as social work, especially the area that social casework and psychosocial work regard as theirs.

These points of contact have also been the reason for competition at various periods of time. Dissociation from psychology on the part of social work originates in the attempts made by social work to develop as a discipline of its own and as a practical activity. This dissociation has varied in scope and strength depending on how possible and desirable the driving forces have considered it to create a distinctive profile for social work in relation to psychology. Through the establishment of institutions of social work at universities, and particularly through the development of psychosocial work as theory and method, social work has taken important steps to give itself a profile as a discipline of its own.

The development of psychosocial work is a necessity for social work, and progress has been made in the direction of developing an independent theoretical base for psychosocial work. There is also good reason to believe that psycho-social work will develop on other theoretical bases than those used so far. A very important consequence of this as far as this study is concerned is that social work as a discipline will have more and more chance of asserting itself within the area of knowledge defined as 'from theory to practice' and 'social problems are generated at the individual level'. This field of knowledge has traditionally been one where the discipline of psychology has been predominant. But by tackling the task of developing its own theoretical concepts, such as psychosocial work for instance, social work will create for itself a natural space within the field of knowledge in question.

Chapter 6
Jane Addams and Social Work

'Jane Addams herself had no taste for self-sacrifice and no condescension, it might be added, toward the poor. Hull House, as she conceived it, did not represent a renunciation of the world. It was not even principally a form of good works. It aimed not so much at helping the poor as at understanding them; and by understanding them, at bridging the chasm that industrialism had opened between social classes. Observation and analysis, therefore, were built into the enterprise from the beginning' (Lasch 1965).

Introduction
On the basis of the theoretical frame of reference presented in Chapter 2, I shall here discuss the fourth and last field in the history of ideas with Jane Addams as an illustration. The field in question in the four-field table is characterised by the variables 'from practice to theory' and 'society generates social problems'.

It is within this field of characteristics that we find Jane Addams's work and thinking. There are many reasons for choosing just Jane Addams for a closer study of the field characterised by 'from practice to theory' and by the causes of social problems being found in society. Jane Addams was the practitioner who started The Settlement Movement as a speciality in social work (see, for example, Davis 1967, Levine 1971). The Settlement Movement constitutes an important background to social work at the group and society levels when it comes to the history of ideas.

Jane Addams is an outstanding pioneer in this tradition in the history of ideas; she paved the way for, and initiated, working methods in social work. In this chapter, I mainly investigate the question of how Jane Addams's work contributes to the development of social work from the standpoint of the 'from practice to theory' tendency in the history of ideas, and the fact that the causes of social problems are to be sought in society, as formulated in the theoretical frame of reference in my study.

Her life history
Jane Addams was born in 1860 in Cedarville, Illinois. She was the youngest of eight children, and their mother died when Jane was barely three years old. John Addams, Jane's father, remarried five years later. He was a prominent person in the state of Illinois and was, among other things, a colleague and close friend of Abraham Lincoln. Father and daughter were very close to each

other, and from her father Jane Addams inherited quickness of mind and a feeling for personal integrity. The father wanted his daughter to make a career for herself and when she was 17 she was sent to Rockford Seminary (later Rockford College), which was situated close to Cedarville. One of the school's specialities was missionary work, and her teachers recommended Jane Addams to take this up. After long discussions and opposition from various quarters, she succeeded in starting medical studies in 1881 at the Women's Medical College in Philadelphia. After a short time, however, she was forced to give up her studies because of a serious back problem which was to plague her all her life.

In the summer of 1883, she made her first journey to Europe. She visited several European countries – Great Britain, Ireland, Germany, Switzerland, France, Greece and Italy – and stayed a long time in London, Berlin and Paris before returning to America in the spring of 1885. It was on this trip that she first came into contact with Toynbee Hall in London, which gave her the idea for what was later to become Hull House in Chicago, founded in 1889 and the most outstanding example of the American Settlement Movement. Addams devoted her life to social work, especially work in society within the framework of The Settlement Movement. As we shall see in a later section, her work encompassed a wide spectrum of activities. After a long period of illness, she went to Russia in 1896 to meet Leo Tolstoy, whose books she had read. Her meeting with Tolstoy was bewildering and thought provoking in many ways. During her stay, she had a chance of testing her thoughts against those of Tolstoy and his perception of society, especially as regards the involvement of the (intellectual) individual in the work of social change. Tolstoy was not impressed by Jane Addams. The well-known writer was, as usual, wearing simple working clothes when he met her and he could not understand why she was so elegantly dressed! He was surprised that Addams could not eat ordinary porridge and also by the fact that she was the absentee landlady of a property in Illinois. Addams felt humiliated by Tolstoy's attitude. On her way back to America she thought that she would have to start baking her own bread and learn from the poor. But no sooner had she arrived back in Chicago than she thought this attitude absurd.

Baking one's own bread was an antiquated doctrine for a very busy social worker. No, she could not work like Tolstoy. 'Compassion was different – it had to be different – in Chicago, in America', as Robert Wuthnow puts it in his book *Acts of Compassion* (1991). Because of her social commitment to Hull House and The Settlement Movement, Jane Addams was called 'the mother of society', and her deep commitment to the peace movement in connection with the First World War gave her the title 'the mother of peace'.

The outbreak of war in Europe in 1914 came as a shock to people who were involved in the problems of society. Their hopes of creating social equality were crushed by the commencement of hostilities. Many activists in The Settlement Movement switched the focus of their activities from national reform work to international peace issues, in which Jane Addams became active. In September 1914, she led a peace meeting at Henry Street Settlement where social workers and reformists discussed the consequences of the war and the responsibility of social workers to support peace. This meeting was to be the beginning of The American Union Against Militarism, and later the Civil Liberties Union. During the same period, Addams headed another organisation, Women's Peace Party, and from 1919 she was also active in the Women's International League for Peace and Freedom. Jane Addams worked very extensively as a peace activist, both nationally and internationally. Her work for peace was considered by many, especially the Establishment in the United States, to be almost anti-American. The years during and around the war were a difficult testing time for Addams's perseverance. As early as 1907, she had published the book *Newer Ideals of Peace* and put forward her ideas on how social responsibility and social ethics should and could be used in peace work. Her work with the various groups of immigrants at Hull House had to a considerable degree formed the basis of the position she took on the involvement of the United States in the war. Her stand for German immigrants, for example, and against American participation in the war against Germany presented her with difficult moral problems. When she was awarded the Nobel Peace Prize in 1931, it was an acknowledgement of her achievements as a peace activist.

Jane Addams died in 1935.

Hull House and the settlement movement
The foundation of Hull House

Jane Addams is best known for having started and run the first, longest-lasting and most extensive settlement in America – Hull House. Those who initiated The Settlement Movement considered that the source of most of the social problems that existed in the growing industrial and urbanised society lay in the environment. Living together with the poor, sharing their conditions of life, their joys and their sorrows meant being a good neighbour. The settlement workers looked upon themselves as good neighbours and not as charity workers; they moved into housing areas with a high degree of social problems.

Jane Addams got the idea that was to become Hull House in London in connection with her first two trips to Europe. On Christmas Eve 1884, two Oxford students had moved into a half-finished building in the slums of East London.

Their purpose was to live there and get to know about the conditions of life in the world of the poor, and to convey some of their knowledge to the slum dwellers. These two students were the first settlement workers, and the half-finished Toynbee Hall the first settlement (Davis 1967). The building took its name from another Oxford student who had lived in the London slums. Samuel A Barnett, who was one of the two students who moved in, called his scheme Practical Socialism, but the emphasis in the activities of Toynbee Hall was on education, since conveying university knowledge to the working class was in itself thought to be an important objective. Barnett tried to develop communication between different classes of society and to revive humanism and the aesthetics of life. The settlement organised art exhibitions, university Extra-Mural Studies, and special lectures.

The settlement idea and Toynbee Hall had inspired many Americans, who with growing concern devoted themselves to the social problems of the industrial and urbanised society. Stanton Coit, who had spent three months at Toynbee Hall in 1886, was the first American to borrow the settlement idea. Together with some friends, he moved into Lower East Side, New York, in August 1886. In order to reform society his maxim was the necessity to organise the intellectual lives and morality of the people. To achieve this aim, the local population would be organised in neighbourhood guilds, each of which was made up of 100 families. Coit moved to Great Britain in 1887 and his grand plans fell through. As the reader will notice, Coit's ideas bore some resemblance to Charles Fourier's Utopian society models of the nineteenth century. The Settlement Movement did not disappear with Coit's failure; it was more than a one-man enterprise and grew in several places at the same time. Another settlement, the Henry Street Settlement (see Wald 1915), was formed in 1893 by Lilian Wald and Mary Brewster.

When Jane Addams visited Toynbee Hall and, together with Ellen Gates Starr, a classmate from Rockford College, founded Hull House she already knew that she would work for social justice. The visit, and above all her experience of poverty in London, left its mark. In her first book about Hull House, Addams depicts a scene from East London that had made an impression on her. During her visit she landed up in the middle of an auction, where late on a Saturday evening fruit and vegetables were being auctioned off, since, on account of the laws in force, they could not be sold until Monday.

> *'On Mile End Road, from the top of an omnibus which paused at the end*
> *of a dingy street lighted by only occasional flares of gas, we saw huge*

masses of ill-clad people clamoring around two hucksters' carts. They were bidding their farthings and ha'pennies for a vegetable held up by the auctioneer, which he at last scornfully flung, with a gibe for its cheapness, to the successful bidder. In the momentary pause only one man detached himself from the groups. He had bidden in a cabbage, and when it struck his hand, he instantly sat down on the curb, tore it with his teeth, and hastily devoured it, unwashed and uncooked as it was. . . They were huddled into ill-fitting, cast-off clothing, the ragged finery which one sees only in East London. Their pale faces were dominated by that most unlovely of human expressions. . .' (Addams 1910:67-68).

It was also during Jane Addams's visit to London that the Pall Mall Gazette wrote about poverty and social misery in London to awaken the conscience of England. These articles also affected Jane Addams. In the summer of 1892, that is, three years after the founding of Hull House, Addams gave a lecture in which she presented her motives for the establishment of The Settlement Movement. She gives three reasons for her involvement in the movement in general and Hull House in particular. The first is 'the desire to make the entire social organism democratic, to extend democracy beyond its political expression'. The second is 'the impulse to share the race life, and to bring as much as possible of social energy and the accumulation of civilization to those portions of the race which have little'. The third is 'a certain renaissance of Christianity' (Lasch 1965). When Addams summarises her motives for settlement work, she produces the early values of her childhood and adolescence and combines these with her need to get out into public life. Addams belonged to the first generation of American women to receive university education at the same time as public career opportunities were more or less closed to them. They were themselves, however, convinced that they had a mission to improve the world. Jill Conway (1964:248-249) writes the following about this:

'No woman of this generation more clearly represents the predicament and its resolution than does Jane Addams. She had a mind whose brilliance and driving power made her acutely responsive to the intellectual and cultural forces of nineteenth-century America. Her personality was characterized by an extreme drive to power which she recognized and strove to discipline from early youth. Intellect made it impossible to accept the achievement of a philistine Chicago, while her complex personality demanded exceptional performance in any task she chose. Since Chicago was the milieu in which she chose to work out her demanding predicament, her solution was one of activism of epic proportions.'

In January 1889, Jane Addams began to look for a suitable housing area in which to form a settlement in Chicago. She consulted many people and went round to many different places to find a suitable building, and finally chose a house in Halsted Street. The then owner of the house became interested in the settlement idea and eventually put the whole house at their disposal. The settlement, which became the most famous in that tradition, was called Hull House after its first owner, Charles J Hull, who built it in 1856. The house was situated in a real slum area. Halsted Street was very neglected and in it there lived mainly unemployed and poor immigrants from Germany, Italy, Poland and Russia. The house was put in order and the two enthusiastic settlement workers moved in on 18 September 1889.

Working principles at Hull House
In the beginning, the guiding principles for settlement work were not very clear. As time went on, work at Hull House developed a more definite form. The aims of the settlement were set out in a declaration: 'To provide a center for a higher civic and social life; to institute and maintain educational and philanthropic enterprises, and to investigate and improve the conditions in the industrial districts of Chicago' (Linn 1935). Addams (1910 and 1930) has given an account of the activities and working methods in two books. What working principles and working methods were shaped at Hull House?

The working principles formulated by Jane Addams and Hull House activists can be summarised in six points (Brieland 1990): (1) settling in the housing area of the needy; (2) personal contact with the inhabitants of the neighbourhood; (3) the importance of aesthetics; (4) no moralising; (5) causes of social problems lie in society; (6) the need for research.

Settling in the housing area of the needy. One of the most central principles of the settlement movement was the settling itself in housing areas where those in need of help lived. The settlement workers were to live among the people they would work for; they would not only be available during office hours or during the time a certain development project was running. The objective was to reduce the social distance between different classes of society. Many of the women at Hull House, for example Edith and Grace Abbott, Sophonisba Breckinridge, Frances Hackett, Alice Hamilton, Florence Kelley, Mary Kenny, Julia Lathrop, Frances Perkins and Ellen Gates Starr had not previously seen poverty. Jane Addams (1910) quotes Samuel A Barnett, founder of Toynbee Hall: 'The things which make men alike are finer and better than the things that keep them apart, and . . . these basic likenesses, if they are properly accentuated, easily transcend the less essential differences of race, language, creed and tradition.'

Linked to this principle was the principle that they should get to know those they were to work for. The inhabitants of Hull House knew the people of the district and considered them their neighbours. They believed that people who know one another trust one another. Jane Addams was also of the opinion that scientific social work must build on people's reciprocity. The social worker must have self-knowledge and must understand the motives they have for choosing the profession of social worker. Another important principle in this context was that the social worker must understand the clients and their unspoken aspirations (see, for example, Elson 1954).

The importance of aesthetics. The settlement workers wanted to change and improve the aesthetic design of the dilapidated housing areas. Changes in the inner and outer environment were a part of settlement work. In the early days at Hull House they started artistic activities such as painting, music and drama. The first new building constructed as an extension to the settlement was an art gallery, where the settlement's first art exhibition was opened in 1891. This and subsequent exhibitions were well attended by the inhabitants of the district. The exhibitions broke the isolation of many immigrants, who did not have very much contact with American life. Addams tells of an Italian immigrant who was surprised that Americans should be interested in art. He had believed that art was something you could only find in Italy and that Americans only thought of dollars. Hull House organised art classes, a music school and theatre performances. Right from the start they had arranged music classes. Hull House Music School was opened in 1893 and provided advanced musical tuition to a limited number of children. Attempts were made to improve the aesthetics of the outer environment by arranging for refuse collection, by building playgrounds, making pavements, and so on.

From moral certainty to rational thinking. When Donna L Franklin (1986) compares Mary Richmond's and Jane Addams's contributions to the development of social work, she chooses the subheading 'From Moral Certainty to Rational Inquiry in Social Work Practice' for her article. The comparison between these two practitioners and thinkers brings out what distinguishes them from one another. When we compare The Settlement Movement with the friendly visitors upon whom Richmond built her casework, what stands out is that The Settlement Movement refrained from moralising and thought that the causes of social problems could be identified in the environment, while the friendly visitors often moralised and considered the individual to be the source of social problems. These differing attitudes were also the source of the controversy between Jane Addams and Mary Richmond, and the reason for Franklin's choice of subheading. Both The Settlement Movement and The Charity Organization Society grew out of English welfare models whose purpose was to solve problems such as poverty, criminality, mental and physical handicaps.

The Settlement Movement stressed the importance of settling among the people to be helped. It was also important to reduce the social distance between helper and those in need of help from different classes of society. The main task of the friendly visitor was to act as a gatekeeper and decide who deserved help. Friendly visitors decided that beggars who were too lazy to work, alcoholics, prostitutes, and other 'immoral' deviants did not qualify to receive help.

The Charity Organization Society (COS) developed from a wish to put the distribution of alms to the poor on a more scientific and efficient basis. The basic attitude of COS was that poverty should be fought by means of personal rehabilitation and not by handing out social welfare. The fundamental philosophy was that poverty could be eliminated by studying the personalities of the poor and thereby rehabilitate them. Friendly visitors were met by hostility and indifference from the poor – they came from well-off districts and belonged to another class and ethnic group.

The founders of The Settlement Movement chose instead to live and work among poor people who were looked upon as neighbours. They tried to show good will by their work in solving problems. Problems were defined in terms of social factors, and they became involved in influencing society. Jane Addams refused to call her neighbours clients or cases and could not fully respect younger social workers who worked an eight-hour day and lived far from the slums. This attitude was consistent with her devotion to learning from her neighbours, as well as with the fact that she corrected the mistakes the 'social workers' had made due to their cultural insensitivity (see Franklin 1986, Pottick 1989).

These differing fundamental attitudes also led to controversy on a personal level between Addams and Richmond. Their first encounter occurred at the National Conference of Charities and Corrections in 1897. Addams (Franklin 1986:509-510) expressed herself as follows:

> *'[the visitors] are bound to tell a man he must be thrifty in order to keep his family. . . You must tell him that he is righteous and a good citizen when he is self-supporting, that he is unrighteous and not a good citizen*

*when he receives aid . . . settlements see that a man may perhaps be a bit
lazy and be a good man and an interesting person . . . it does not lay so
much stress on one set of virtues, but views the man in his social
aspects'.*

When Addams had finished her address, Richmond countered immediately
and characterised the settlements as 'like old-fashioned missions, doing harm
by their cheap, sprinkling sort of charity' (Franklin 1986).

Jane Addams's starting point, then, was that the causes of social problems were
to be sought in people's surroundings, that is, in society. On this matter, she
followed John Dewey, pragmatist, philosopher and sociologist, and a close
friend of Addams and of Hull House, who argued that people's interests and
values were shaped by their environment and not by inborn factors (see Lasch
1965, Greenstone 1979, Franklin 1986, Deegan 1988). While Dewey's standpoint was a basic assumption built on the ideas of pragmatism, Addams found
her actual examples in her immediate surroundings. Poverty and social
problems were a consequence of people's education, occupation, housing
situation, and so on. The fact that they were thieves or prostitutes had nothing
to do with their personalities or factors in the individual, but was a result of
their position in the social structure.

The use of research in The Settlement Movement. Hull House was first and
foremost a settlement where they carried on practical work of social change.
Rather early in the development of the settlement, they pointed out the importance of social research in the work of change (see, for example, Fish 1985).
During the first decades after the founding of Hull House, social work was
undeveloped. Compilation of systematic statistics of social conditions was
rare and sociology had only just started to become a discipline. Hull House
carried out their own investigations into the social conditions of the district.
Their main areas of investigation were working conditions in factories,
housing conditions, health and the presence of different diseases in the district,
alcohol and drug misuse, children's education and pedagogical problems. The
research reports were used to gain an understanding of the bad conditions they
wanted to change and to support their arguments in discussions with politicians
and decision-making bodies. Several of the Hull House activists also had connections with the University of Chicago, whose ambition was to use Hull
House as a kind of field research station. The best-known research report in
this connection is *Hull House Maps and Papers* (Holmberg 1978), written by a
group of Hull House activists.

Working methods at Hull House

How did they work at Hull House? What were the main working areas? Brieland (1990) divides Hull House activities into three areas/functions: direct social service, educational and leisure activities, and social reforms.

Direct social service was one of the most important areas of work. They worked with the needs of the inhabitants of the district, which could include a broad spectrum of personal needs. Direct social service was normally provided without any planning, as the needs arose and as a one-off occurrence. When somebody needed help of some kind, they tried to give them that help. They tried to avoid making value judgements about those seeking help. Much of the help that was provided was directed towards raising people's ability to help themselves. Addams wrote, for example, in *Twenty Years at Hull House* (1910:167):

'We early found ourselves spending many hours in efforts to secure support for deserted women, insurance for bewildered widows, damages for injured operators, furniture from the clutches of the instalment store. The Settlement is valuable as an information and interpretation bureau. It constantly acts between the various institutions of the city and the people for whose benefit these institutions were erected. The hospitals, the county agencies, and State asylums are often but vague rumors to the people who need them most. Another function of the Settlement to its neighborhood resembles that of the big brother whose mere presence on the playground protects the little one from bullies.'

Educational and leisure activities were another area developed by Hull House. Over the years, the Hull House activists carried out many schemes for changing the negative social conditions in the housing area. Educational and leisure activities were group practices. This work consisted in development programmes which were later in social work to be called group work and neighbourhood work. They included many different types of activities. In her account of the work at Hull House, Addams gives many examples of what group work could involve. They built, for example, gymnasiums and playgrounds where children and young people were organised in groups and participated in social activities. Education was also arranged for children, with the aim of raising their level of social maturity. Otherwise these children would have attended overcrowded schools, which would consequently not have been able to give them a satisfactory upbringing.

Social reforms. In her book *Twenty Years at Hull House*, Addams writes about two reform issues that occupied a lot of the Hull House activists' time and taxed their strength during the first 20 years: conditions on the labour market and juvenile courts.

Working conditions were extremely bad; the workers had hardly any rights and no security at the turn of the century in the United States. Addams and her colleagues became aware of the shocking conditions when they first settled at Hull House. She described how dramatic and upsetting their encounter with the workers' bad working conditions was. On the first Christmas Eve at Hull House, some young girls were offered sweets, but refused them and said that they had been working at a sweet factory from seven in the morning until nine in the evening for six weeks, so they could not even stand the sight of sweets. Addams and her colleagues, who did not know very much about child labour, were shocked. They were distressed when three boys from one of the Hull House clubs were injured at a factory, one of them fatally. Working conditions for adults were no better. The most outstanding problem could be described by the term 'sweated labour', which stood for very bad working conditions and starvation wages in the clothing industry. The families of the district suffered a lot because of the sweating system, which was organised by small businesses in competition with the large employers in the clothing industry.

Hull House fought for many years against child labour and sweating, and forced the authorities to undertake several social reforms that improved conditions of life for the inhabitants. 'Sweaters', who employed men, women and children, supplied the clothing industry with clothes of different kinds. There were about 25,000 to 30,000 people of different ethnic groups working in Chicago's sweating system, and they sought employment with sweaters from their own ethnic groups. The reforms that were implemented included scientific investigations of working conditions, the formation of four trade unions, legislation on working conditions, particularly on working hours for women and children, and inspection of working conditions in factories. Florence Kelley of Hull House achieved a lot here, especially when she was appointed first factory inspector in the State of Illinois.

The other big issue was the setting up of juvenile courts. With the aim of separating the handling of juvenile delinquents from heavy crime among adults, a juvenile court was established in Chicago in 1889. Julia Lathrop of Hull House was very active in this work. The court was situated close to Hull House; a 'psychopathic' section was started as well to work with psychiatric questions. During the same period, the Juvenile Protective Association was formed to work with juvenile delinquents and with young people on the verge of criminal activity. The 22 workers in the association met at Hull House every week. The model for dealing with juvenile criminality developed by Hull House eventually spread to other parts of Illinois and later to other American states.

To sum up, we can say that Hull House and The Settlement Movement around Hull House had the work of social change as their primary objective. The Hull House activities comprised personal social service, group and neighbourhood work, mainly in the form of educational and leisure activities, and working for structural change in the form of social reforms. Addams and The Settlement Movement developed by her held the fundamental view that social problems were generated by conditions in society and that they had nothing to do with the personality of the individual. In addition, it was considered that the work of social change must be based on scientific knowledge, and this is discussed in the next section.

Basing practice on scientific knowledge
During her career, Jane Addams wrote a considerable amount. Her works include many articles and several books. She also had a tendency to quote herself, which means that her texts were published several times in various contexts. Her work comprises various types of text which can on the whole be divided into the following categories: (1) standpoints on philosophical and moral questions; (2) descriptions of Hull House and its activities; (3) scientific texts, that is, surveys of social conditions; (4) peace issues. Jane Addams did not publish any collected theoretical work that discusses the theoretical and scientific foundations of settlement work. Mostly her works were disparate which, when taken together, can be regarded as descriptions of practice, that is, descriptions of the settlement activities on the one hand and *attempts* at theorising around the questions generated by this practice on the other. A comprehensive presentation of her published works cannot be given within the limits of the present study, but some strategically chosen works will be focused on here. The core work in this connection is *Hull House Maps and Papers* (Addams 1895).

Hull House Maps and Papers
The book entitled *Hull House Maps and Papers* (hereafter referred to as HHMP) includes two colour maps showing demographic characteristics of the inhabitants of the district. One of these maps shows the ethnic composition of the population, which comprised 18 ethnic groups ('nationalities'). The other map is a compilation of the population's housing conditions, occupations and wages. As Jane Addams wrote in the introduction (HHMP 1895), she had got the idea from Charles Booth's (1902) London studies made during the period

1892-1897. The maps were a novelty in the USA and made excellent pedagogical aids for informing both decision-makers and the inhabitants themselves. Enlarged copies of the maps hung at times on the walls of Hull House. The ten chapters of the book dealt with the issues of most immediate interest in the district.

The first chapter, written by Agnes Sinclair Holbrook, deals with questions of methods used in the study, and also contains an ethnogeographical description of the district. That the study was made as a foundation on which to base the work of social change can be clearly seen from the way it is drawn up. Holbrook wrote about the aims of the study:

> *'While vitally interested in every question connected with this part of the city, and especially concerned to enlarge the life and vigor of the immediate neighborhood, Hull House offers these facts more with the hope of stimulating inquiry and* **action***, and evolving new thoughts and methods, than with the idea of recommending its own manner of effort'* (HHMP 1895:13; emphasis added).

Data had been collected by means of a simple questionnaire developed by Florence Kelley, who administered 'a special investigation of the slums of great cities' for the United States Department of Labor. A detailed description of the working method is presented in the chapter, including how the area is delimited, data-collection instruments, questions of categorisation, and so on. The presentation is simple in comparison with today's sophisticated method discussions, but includes the most basic relevant elements. There is also an ethnogeographical and sociological description of the area, which included one of Chicago's most criminal and poorest districts. Besides dwellings, small workshops and shops there were three factories in the area.

In addition to the introduction to the book and an appendix on Hull House, Jane Addams herself wrote a chapter on the importance of The Settlement Movement to the working class movement. Addams regarded the trade unions mainly as a positive force which organised the workers, created awareness of social changes in a historical perspective, and stressed co-operation between the workers instead of competition and conflict. She distanced herself, however, from militant acts. She considered the settlement to be a forum where the working class movement and the trade unions could be mobilised. This chapter came to be an important basis for Addams's later texts on the working-class movement and the trade unions.

From a sociological point of view, the most impressive chapters are written by Florence Kelley and deal with the exploitation of workers – men, women and children. The so-called sweating system is described with scientific precision and analytical acuity. The conditions described in Kelley's two chapters were present during several years and used to form a knowledge base for Hull House activities aimed at helping and mobilising the inhabitants in their struggle against bad working and labour market conditions.

Three chapters in the book deal with ethnic minorities and immigrants. Charles Zeublin, later to become one of the leading sociologists of the Chicago School, wrote about conditions of life for the Jewish group. The uniting force of the Jewish community was a mainstay of everyday life, despite the fact that the Jewish workers lived in extreme conditions of poverty. Two other ethnic groups specially studied were Italian and Bohemian immigrants, and a chapter was devoted to each of them in the book.

Yet another of interest was written by Julia Lathrop, and described the deplorable conditions in social institutions in the Cook district.

Even if Jane Addams wrote only a limited part of the book, it was she, together with Florence Kelley, who planned and ran the project. The purpose of the book was to provide scientific facts that would be used in the work of social change. *Hull House Maps and Papers*, more than any other book of Addams (and the Hull House settlement), marks the importance of research as a base for the work of social change. Mary Jo Deegan (1988b:62), who wrote an extremely polemical book on Jane Addams and male dominance over the sociology of the Chicago School, ascribed great importance to this book:

'HH Maps and Papers *established the following precedents: the use of mapping as a statistical technique to reveal patterns of social groups; emphasis on the city as a factor structuring daily lives; the analysis of immigrant groups and their disorganization in the city, primarily as a function of debilitating economic conditions; and a direct link between the work of Hull-House residents and sociologists at Chicago.*

'*The authors of HH Maps and Papers also differed from the male Chicago School in that (1) they stressed economic conditions as a major cause of social problems that needed to be altered; (2) they studied art as a function of everyday life; (3) they often focused on the study of women;*

*(4) they advocated direct social changes such as government interven-
tion for the needy or labor organizing, and (5) they decried conflict as a
method of social interaction and did not believe it was the basis of
society or social order.'*

Hull House Maps and Papers marked the importance of social research as the
first step in the work of social change and social reforms. The scientific
methods used in their research work were social, scientific or sociological.
These methods and models used in *Hull House Maps and Papers* were further
developed by the Chicago School of Sociology. Jane Addams and The
Settlement Movement, therefore, did not introduce their own specific methods
and models to the work of social change but strongly stressed the importance of
the use of the methods of the social sciences. It is also an indication that social
work is a growing profession and discipline among the other social sciences.

Standpoints on philosophical and moral issues

Jane Addams formulated her philosophical and moral standpoints, which form
the foundations of her practical and theoretical work, in a number of books.

Democracy and Social Ethics (1902) summarises her views on philosophical
and moral issues. The book consists of seven articles that she had earlier
published in a number of periodicals after first having presented them in
speeches and addresses on various occasions. Her standpoints, or basic
assumptions, can be summarised as follows: (1) people are dependent on each
other; (2) all people are of equal value, regardless of race, creed, ethnic origin,
gender, and so on; (3) people can only develop fully in a society that recognises
their mutual dependence and that provides the necessary democratic rules; (4)
ideas and thoughts are dependent on experience.

Jane Addams was deeply influenced by John Dewey's thinking (see, for
example, Greenstone 1975, Fish 1985, Franklin 1986, Deegan 1981 and 1988b)
Dewey was a pragmatist who believed in the profound importance of science and
empiricism in human development and changes in society. Knowledge was not
the sum of a number of truths but a product of investigations that were ongoing
processes. Knowledge of specific phenomena was not final and complete. The
basic assumptions of pragmatism also led to the belief that people who lived in
poverty could not be blamed for their predicament but were under the influence
of societal factors. Experience and practice were the foundations of all
knowledge. They were also the grounds of legitimacy for good and evil. You
could know what was good and what was evil through experience.

Addams always used her own experience as her base and expressed concrete ideas at the same time as she tried to find generalities. Many of her texts are examples of her working method, namely *autobiographical*. In the autobiography, she recounts her experiences, which are often also discussed more theoretically. In spite of this, she never arrived at a more-general theory of society and social action.

In her attempt to point out the negative aspects of charity, she emphasises the importance of democratic values. She wrote, for example, in *Democracy and Social Ethics* (1902:13-14):

'Our conceptions of morality, as all our other ideas, pass through a course of development; the difficulty comes in adjusting our conduct, which has become hardened into customs and habits, to these changing moral conceptions. When this adjustment is not made, we suffer from the strain and indecision of believing one hypothesis and acting upon another.

'Probably there is no relation in life which our democracy is changing more rapidly than the charitable relation – that relation which obtains between benefactor and beneficiary; at the same time there is no point of contact in our modern experience which reveals so clearly the lack of that equality which democracy implies. . . . the very need and existence of charity, denies us the consolation and freedom which democracy will at last give.'

In the same text, and linked to the question of democratic rights, relations between social classes are discussed; between the poor and needy of the working class on the one hand and representatives of the middle and upper classes who devote themselves to charity on the other. Addams brings out the cultural differences between the working class and the middle class. The working class, who live under a definite set of economic and social circumstances, have developed a culture that differs from that of the middle class. These differences make it more difficult for social workers from the middle classes to understand the problems of the working classes and the factors that lie behind these problems. The general opinion among the friendly visitors and social workers of that time was that the poor are lazy and depraved, and the reason was that it was difficult for the middle classes to realise what cultural and social differences there are between the classes. It was precisely this argument that is developed in *Democracy and Social Ethics* and that motivates settlement: the act of settling among the needy with the aim of reducing the social distance between the classes.

Addams: sociologist, social worker, and settlement worker

In several works (1978, 1981, 1988a, 1988b, 1990), Mary Jo Deegan has studied American sociologists, particularly female ones, working within or in connection with the Chicago School. Her largest and most extensive work came out in 1988 and is called *Jane Addams and the Men of the Chicago School* 1892-1918 (1988b), in which she argues that studies of urban conditions within the Chicago School started as early as the 1890s and that these studies were initiated by Chicago sociologists, mainly women and supporters of reform, led by Jane Addams. Jane Addams's substantial contributions to the development of sociology in the Chicago School were ignored and relegated to the backyard of history in the 1920s by male sociologists who were non-political and anti- reformist sexists.

The fact that Deegan (1990) perceives Jane Addams as 'the greatest sociologist of her day' and 'a social theorist of major proportions' leads us to pay attention to her study. Was Jane Addams a *sociologist* or a *social worker*? Or was she a *settlement worker*?

Deegan sets up five criteria that argue in favour of Addams being a sociologist. These criteria are (1) that one holds a professorship in sociology or teaches sociology; (2) that one is a member of the National Association of Sociologists; (3) that one is a writer of sociological articles or textbooks; (4) that one considers oneself to be a sociologist; (5) that one is defined as a sociologist by others. Deegan is of the opinion that one is a sociologist if one fulfils one of the five criteria, and claims that Addams fulfils all five.

Addams taught on several courses in sociology. She was twice offered a post at the department of sociology at the University of Chicago but turned it down both times. She wanted to remain outside the academy and devote herself to adult education for those who could not enter the university. She was a member of the American Sociological Society when it was founded in 1905 and was active until 1930. Addams published five articles in the *American Journal of Sociology* (1896, 1905, 1908, 1912, 1914). Deegan believes that *Hull House Maps and Papers* and *Democracy and Social Ethics* were two important sociological works – especially, the latter was 'a major sociological and theoretical statement on the construction of social order and its meaning'.

Deegan claims that Addams refused to adopt formal titles and that she felt herself compelled to be called the 'head' of the Hull House settlement. Despite her resistance to formal titles, she perceived herself as a sociologist, Deegan (1990) thinks, and quotes Farell: 'Miss Addams later identified herself professionally with these sociologists. In 1908 she wrote of her attendance at the

American Sociological Association: "I simply have to take care of my professional interests once in a while and this little trip was full of inspiration".'

Deegan also states that Addams was held in high esteem by the sociologists of the Chicago School, and by others outside it as well. Hull House was a central institution for female sociologists from 1892 until the 1920s, and during this period the Hull House activists worked together with men from the University of Chicago. They created a foundation for American sociology and *Hull House Maps and Papers* marks the intellectual birth of the Chicago School of Sociology.

Issues such as the social consequences of urbanisation, the sociocultural lifestyles of immigrants, and economic factors affecting the community were at the core of the work undertaken by the Hull House activists. They also developed maps describing various aspects of social conditions among the local population. It is the Hull House activists who deserve the credit for all these things, according to Deegan.

Deegan does not characterise Jane Addams as a social worker, even if she (Deegan) describes the social processes that resulted in many female sociologists being transferred to social work at the University of Chicago during the 1920s.

The Hull House women thought of social work as an instrument for what Deegan calls 'critical pragmatism' and 'cultural feminism'. In other cities and at other universities, social workers were more psychology oriented in both their theory and practice. The social workers in Chicago perceived themselves as 'change agents' and as critics of the social order, not its representatives.

According to Deegan, two essential professional changes of importance to female sociologists were taking place in 1918. Sociology was on its way towards abandoning its former research ideals, its role in society and its institutional attitude towards involvement outside the academic world. Social work was just about to legitimise its academic existence, something that sociology, for its part, had already as good as done. For social work, these changes had come about in connection with changes in the academic world and on account of social consequences of the First World War. As academic sociologists more and more defined 'applied sociology' as social work, social workers took the chance to raise their professional status. Many female sociologists had already become identified with social work, at the same time as they were marginalised in the male sociology profession.

Mary Jo Deegan reaches very definite conclusions: Jane Addams was the greatest sociologist of her time and led a group of female sociologists with their headquarters at Hull House. Addams, through her work, laid the foundations of what came to be called the Chicago School of Sociology, with a mainly urban-sociological orientation. Jane Addams and her female colleagues were erased from the history of sociology on account of their uncomfortable ideas and attitudes, which were disapproved of by the Chicago sociological Establishment. Some of the women moved into social work, which was regarded as applied sociology. In contrast to social workers and social work academics at other universities, these women looked upon themselves as change agents.

Mary Jo Deegan's line of reasoning has met with strong opposition from some quarters. Dmitri Shalin (1990) finds Deegan's thesis exaggerated and does not consider her argumentation convincing. His view is that it is important to note that the Hull House type of sociology was not practised only and mainly by women. The proof presented in his book shows that many male sociologists from the University of Chicago were active in Hull House sociology.

Martin Bulmer, a sociologist and the author of a comprehensive book on the Chicago School, is even more severe in his judgement. He considers Deegan's argumentation and analytical approach to be unsatisfactory. She is trying to prove a predetermined thesis, he thinks (1989:1480), and writes:

> 'This is established at the outset in the author's curious insistence that, despite the fact that she herself did not accept the title, Jane Addams **was** an early American sociologist, who has been unjustly excluded from histories of sociology. The author entirely fails to grapple with the rela- tionship between what George Vincent in 1897 called the philosophical and scientific sides of sociology and the "social technological".
> Addams, Kelley, Abbott, and Breckinridge were representatives of the latter, most closely identified with either the settlement house movement or social work education. . . There is no doubt about their importance in early American social inquiry, much more doubt about the claim that they were really sociologists at a time when sociology was already becoming institutionalized in some universities' (emphasis original).

In an article with the significant heading 'The Hull House Tradition and the Contemporary Social Worker: Was Jane Addams Really a Social Worker?', Donald Brieland (1990) discusses Addams's professional identity. In his presen- tation, Brieland sets up a number of criteria by which to define social work and then poses the question of how these criteria correspond with Jane Addams and the Hull House tradition. The following criteria are used by Brieland: (1) to help people to increase their social competence and their capacity to solve problems; (2) to help people to acquire resources; (3) to make organisations become people-oriented and accessible; (4) to facilitate people's interaction with one another; (5) to influence the interaction between organisations and institutions; (6) to influence social policy.

Jane Addams was reluctant to adopt formal titles and identification labels for herself. Most of all, she avoided calling herself a social worker. In all probability, this was due to the fact that *social work* and *social worker* were terms that came to be used by The Charity Organization Society, which, like Mary Richmond, stood for social work oriented towards the individual – a standpoint that Addams strongly dissociated herself from. However, Addams did call herself a settlement worker on one occasion (*Who's Who in America* 1935).

Regardless of the subjective identification, can we identify Jane Addams as a social worker in the modern sense on the basis of the criteria set up by Brieland? Brieland (1990) comes to this conclusion: 'Perhaps Jane Addams, at an earlier time and in a simpler context, embodied the true social worker better than the inheritors of the helping process.'

Brieland ends his article with some of the fundamental questions in social work today: (1) Are social workers 'neighbours' as well as professionals? (2) Are they educated for preventive work as well as for treating psychosocial problems? (3) Do they work sufficiently with the large issues of society? (4) Should they be social workers in the Addams tradition? (5) Is Addams one of them; are they sufficiently like her?

We can now ask ourselves whether Jane Addams was a sociologist, a social worker, or a settlement worker. The question is really wrongly put. The question is whether we have to choose one or the other. Must Addams be one or the other? On the basis of available research referred to here, there are good reasons for looking upon Jane Addams as being sociologist, social worker, and settlement worker.

In Chapter 2, I discussed problems of delimitation between sociology and social work. I established that there are at least two central points where sociology and social work intersect. One of these is the attitude of these subjects (and professions) towards social problems, and the other is how they see social change and the work of social change. Studies, and the handling, of social problems, and studies of social change and the handling of the work of social change constitute central subject areas that sociology and social work traditionally lay claim to. These are, therefore, issues that lie at the interface of sociology and social work. Jane Addams worked in this border area. She considered that social problems were generated by society and that we must change social conditions to liberate people from social problems. And the best way to perform the work of social change was on the spot, close to the people for whom the work of social change was intended. From this history of ideas perspective, it is not so surprising that Addams is looked upon as a sociologist as well as a social worker and settlement worker.

Discussion

Jane Addams was a practitioner who founded and ran the Hull House settlement in one of Chicago's slum districts. For several decades, Hull House was a centre of social change work. The Hull House activists worked with social programmes which today are defined as group and community work. At an early stage of their activities, the Hull House workers realised that it was essential to support the work of social change with scientific knowledge. Socioscientific research became an integral part of the work of social change carried out at Hull House. This integration, however, did not apply to the total activity of it.

From our presentation above, it can be seen that the activities at Hull House comprised three main areas: direct social service, educational and leisure activities, and social reforms. Research was linked to the involvement of The Settlement Movement in social reforms. On the basis of the assumptions according to which Jane Addams and the Hull House settlement worked, it was natural that they mainly concentrated on finding scientific grounds for their structurally oriented social work. This aim was also in keeping with Addams's relations with sociologists at the University of Chicago.

The Hull House settlement's other fields of work were not particularly well grounded in the production of scientific knowledge. As far as their work in education, specially adult education and leisure activities, was concerned, Hull House was influenced by the ideas of John Dewey, for example. But when it came to direct social service, practical activity and theory were not integrated. Direct social service is a field that can be compared with social work directed at the individual. The individual-oriented social work within the Hull House settlement was carried on in an unsystematic and spontaneous manner, and never attained the worth it deserved. The type of professionalism developed by Mary Richmond and others during the same period was ignored by the settlement activists.

It also meant that direct social service lacked scientific ground and integration. This is naturally connected with the fact that they were little interested in individual-oriented social work in The Settlement Movement. The fact that they chose to settle in districts where the poor and socially deprived lived contributed, however, to their coming into contact on an individual level with needs that required immediate action. They were thus partly forced, and perhaps more or less against their will, to devote themselves to individual-oriented social work without having to ground it in the production of scientific knowledge.

Jane Addams's practical work and thinking have been studied in this chapter from the viewpoint of the theoretical frame of reference on which my book is based. Her practical activities and ideas can be studied in the field of characteristics within the history of ideas that is characterised by 'from practice to theory', and by the causes of social problems being found in society. 'From practice to theory' represents a tendency in the history of ideas which means that practice or the work of social change constitutes the starting point and basis of theoretical knowledge and knowledge development. From practice, the diversity of life, is born the need for theoretical knowledge. There is a desire to explain and understand practice on a more general level. Theoretical activity is integrated into practical activity. In the case of Jane Addams and Hull House, the work of social change is integrated into both the immediate environment and into the sociopolitical field with statistical and sociological surveys and analyses of social problems and conditions. The studies carried out within the framework of the book Hull House Maps and Papers are the most representative example of these efforts.

The theoretical frame of reference of this study also includes another relevant aspect of the history of ideas, namely, the efforts of practitioners and thinkers to understand the character of social problems. From the history of ideas perspective, the causes of social problems have been sought in the individual and in society. Jane Addams and the type of settlement movement she represents are examples of seeking the causes of social problems in society and in people's immediate social environment. This basic assumption is made explicitly clear by at least three factors: (1) In her practical activity and her theoretical ideas, Addams declares that her basic assumption is that social problems have their origin in society. It is, moreover, also an important source of her controversy with Mary Richmond. (2) Jane Addams works constantly with the problem of democracy. Her conception of democracy comprises both political and economic connotations (for these concepts, see Abrahamsson and Broström 1979).

The inequality of society is, according to Addams, the source of most social problems. (3) The choice of focus for the work of social change. Jane Addams considered that it is society in general and the immediate social environment in particular that must be changed if we are to solve social problems.

The work of social change and the production of knowledge on the conditions to be changed are integrated elements in Jane Addams's works. This means that Addams moves within an area of practice that both sociology and social work can lay claim to. This area of practice includes social problems and social change, and constitutes a kind of interface between sociology and social work. The boldest claim I have seen in this context is that made in Mary Deegan's study of Jane Addams. Deegan declares that Addams was 'the greatest sociologist of her day'. It is, on the other hand, noteworthy that the same claim is lacking in the studies that regard Addams as a representative of social work.

That the historians of both sociology and social work formulate their claims about Jane Addams's work at different levels can be due to various reasons. Two possible ones are interesting if we take as our starting point the questions posed in chapter 2. Firstly, could it be that it is so self-evident that Jane Addams is perceived as a social worker, that there is consequently no reason to make bold, explicit claims for her as being a prominent representative of the profession and discipline of social work? Correspondingly, it may not be just as obvious that Jane Addams can be considered 'the greatest sociologist of her day', which means that this claim must be made explicitly and strongly. The other interesting question we should ask is about a discipline's self-confidence and identity as a scientific discipline and profession. Do representatives of social work, including its historians, lack the historical instruments and a greater degree of awareness of the core and limits of the subject to be able to identify clearly, and lay claim to, the central pioneers of the discipline?

Regardless of which discipline lays claim to Jane Addams's work, and regardless of which one succeeds in linking her work to it, we can be sure of two points of departure: (1) Jane Addams's practical work is an early example of what modern social work is engaged in today. Addams's great merit does not rest, however, only on the fact that she paved the way for structurally oriented social work or the work of social change, but that she also integrated the scientific production of knowledge into the work of social change. (2) If Jane Addams is to be seen as a sociologist, her distinctive character and strength lie in her emphasis on the fact that interest in sociological knowledge is to be found in social change. The *raison d'être* of sociological or social scientific knowledge is its use in the work of social change. Her sociology is then an example of it as an agent activity.

Community work and Jane Addams

Community work is today an important part of social work. Community work aims at supporting people so they can organise their lives in order to be able to solve their own problems. This presupposes that the problems are identified and formulated from below, that is, in the first place by the people concerned themselves, with the help of community workers. The role of the social or community worker (as many social workers prefer to call themselves) consists mainly in supporting the process of change with professional working methods. The degree of activity of the community worker and the people involved is the subject of dynamic and mutual influences in which the character of the problem and the initial ability of people to participate in the process of change and conditions in the social environment constitute the main ingredients.

The foundation of ideas underlying modern community work is to be found in The Settlement Movement. The settlement idea came to Sweden relatively early, and the first Swedish settlement was established at Birkagården in 1912. Modern community work, however, has developed from the end of the 1960s. This development followed in the footsteps of new social and semi-political movements that grew up in other parts of Europe and in America. In several countries considered to be welfare states, there was concern about, and dissatisfaction with, social conditions, mainly among groups of intellectuals. They sought the causes of social problems in the structural conditions of society. In this intellectual opposition to conservative forces, there developed social movements that now provide the social and intellectual dynamics for modern community work which goes back to the ideas of The Settlement Movement of the nineteenth century.

Community work is, in the first place, considered to be a working method It is also a perspective on social change. The basic principles of modern community work are to be found in Jane Addams and The Settlement Movement, among others. The basic assumptions of the perspective lie in the fact that social problems are primarily generated by structural conditions in society. The work of change must therefore be directed at conditions in society. People who meet with social problems have a fundamental capacity to do something about their situation. They should receive support and help at different stages of the process of change. This support is provided by community workers, who develop a professional battery of models and methods for change. These basic assumptions, which developed within the framework of The Settlement Movement led by Jane Addams, apply today as well.

Community work as a perspective and working method has to a large extent drawn its theoretical concepts from disciplines such as pedagogy and sociology. However, attempts are being made to define a conceptual field for community work within the framework of the discipline of social work (see, for example, Goetschius 1969, Rothman 1974 and, particularly, Thomas 1983). In the book *Social mobilisering* (1992), a group of writers in Sweden have tried to specify the bounds of community work, especially in the way it has developed in Sweden. The book shows clearly the great need to develop community work as a set of theoretical ideas. Two writers, Olsson and Ronnby, outline in the book some theoretical ways of development for the concept of community work. The former works from Tönnies's two concepts *Gemeinschaft* and *Gesellschaft*, while the latter has adopted a Marxist-inspired approach.

Chapter 7
History of Ideas and Fields of Knowledge

Social work and the history of ideas – a summary

The purpose of my book has been to provide an introductory survey of the roots of the history of ideas in social work. This final chapter will be devoted to linking together some of the arguments developed in the book. I have seen social work as practice and as a scientific discipline. It is social work as a scientific discipline that has been the focus of the work. As discussed in Chapter 1, this was a deliberate choice intended to emphasise the level of ambition of my study. Earlier studies in the history of ideas in social work have concentrated mainly, or at times one-sidedly, on the development of social work as a profession or as an organisation, or attempts have been made to study the history of the subject from the standpoint of man's tendency to facilitate mutual help. This has resulted in social work as practice being emphasised or over-emphasised, at the cost of the development of the subject as a scientific discipline taking second place.

My point of departure has been to look upon social work both as practice and as a scientific discipline. It has therefore been my ambition to ground social work in the analysis of the emergence of social science. In the perspective I have presented, the history of ideas in social work is rooted in the breakthrough of social analysis in the eighteenth-century and, above all, in the predominant nineteenth-century ambitions to use scientific analysis to improve people's social conditions and to eliminate social problems.

The conceptual framework of the study is the theoretical frame of reference, the four-field table, presented in Chapter 2. This theoretical frame of reference includes two variables that capture central elements in the development of the history of ideas in social science, and this is also of special relevance to social work as practice and as a scientific discipline. The one aspect is the interplay of theory and practice and the other is the nature of the causes of social problems. The reader will have become acquainted with these variables. The first variable has been dichotomised by the values 'from theory to practice' and 'from practice to theory'. The second variable has been dichotomised by the values 'society generates social problems' and 'the individual generates social problems'. The four-field table, constructed by cross-tabulating the variables, has been illustrated with central examples from the history of ideas. This survey has shown that there is a very special history-of-ideas relationship between these two variables: the central issue carved out in a history-of-ideas perspective comprises the relationship between theory and practice and the nature of social problems in a context where these two aspects are connected.

The complex of problems around the relationship between theory and practice can be looked at from different perspectives and fields of interest, for example from the viewpoints of the theory of knowledge, philosophy of science or history of ideas. As things have developed in nineteenth-century discussions on the scientific analysis of society and social change, it is a matter of explaining and understanding social phenomena (analysing these scientifically) and using the knowledge gained for social change. In this context, our conception of the nature of social problems is of special importance. Scientific knowledge of society and of man as a social being is to be used for social change, the aim of which is to eliminate social problems and improve people's condition of life. There is thus a logical and historical:empirical relationship between scientific social analysis, social change and social problems. This connection manifests itself at various stages of this study. The study testifies to the fact that the different fields of the theoretical frame of reference are not isolated empirical islands but that there are entrances and exits between the fields when it comes to the evolution of the various ideas.

FIGURE 7.1 The fields of history of ideas in social work

Nature of the causes of social problems

		Society generates social problems	The individual generates social problems
Development of ideas in the interaction between theory and practice	From theory to practice	1 Saint-Simon Agent activity	2 Psychological approaches
	From practice to theory	3 Jane Addams Structural social work	4 Mary Richmond Psychosocial work

With reference to field 1, I focused attention in Chapter 3 on Saint-Simon's work and Saint-Simonism as a phenomenon in the history-of-ideas. This field is characterised by the history of ideas tendency 'from theory to practice' and by the idea that it is society that generates social problems. Scientific analysis is therefore to be used to reveal in what way society generates social problems, and then these problems will be eliminated with the help of this scientific knowledge.

Diagonally opposite this idea is field 4, which I studied in Chapter 4. This field is characterised by the history of ideas tendency 'from practice to theory', and by the fact that it is the individual who generates social problems. From the viewpoint of the history of ideas, this field is an example of the primacy of practice in relation to theoretical development, when the practitioner is of the opinion that social problems are generated by individuals themselves. Therefore, the working procedure is that practice, the work of social change, is directed towards doing something about the social problems of the individual; a process that can also provide more general knowledge through scientific analysis. I have here studied Mary Richmond, whose contribution to the evolution of social work has been followed up by developments belonging to field 2.

Field 2 is characterised by the history-of-ideas tendency 'from theory to practice', and by the fact that the individual is considered to be the source of social problems. Here it is theoretical development that forms the base for social change, with the individual at the centre of attention. Within this field, it is the contribution of psychology to casework as a model of social change that has been studied. I have also shown the competition there was, and still is, between psychology and social work as regards development after Mary Richmond's casework model.

Field 3 is characterised by the history-of-ideas tendency 'from theory to practice', and by the fact that the origin of social problems is to be sought in society. This field has been studied by looking at Jane Addams's contribution to social work.

The relationship between the different parts of the theoretical frame of reference is intricate in that, on the one hand, there is an intimate connection between theory and practice and, on the other, a complicated connection between different levels of analysis as regards the nature of the social problems. What seem to be isolated fields in the four-field table are, in fact, manifestations of complicated ontological relationships and relationships between various ideas in the history of social work. The history-of-ideas contexts studied within the framework of each and every one of these fields are intertwined in a complicated manner, at the same time as each one has its own core of development that can be carved out as a tradition in the history of ideas with its own worth.

Theoretical frames of reference of this type may be thought to constitute unnecessary limitations to research, at the same time as they are indispensable if empirical fields are to be dealt with inside reasonable analytical bounds. One of the points of this theoretical frame of reference is to make it possible to handle a complicated empirical field. Different traditions in the history of ideas are formulated within the framework of the theoretical frame of reference. These are central to the evolution of ideas in social work. In studies (Bruno 1948, Davis 1967, Kahn 1959, Pumphrey 1956, Wald 1915) concentrating on the professional development of social work, work has been carried out in the lower half of the four-fold table; within the framework of the history-of-ideas tendency 'from practice to theory'. These studies, however, have mainly been a one-sided description of the organisational development of the profession. What is unusual in the research into the history of ideas in social work is to probe the 'from theory to practice' tendency and to bring out an overall picture in which different traditions in the history of ideas can be thought to form a common background to the evolution of social work.

Central points of contact between different traditions in the history of ideas have already been discussed in the context of their respective chapters. It is, however, useful in a final chapter to emphasise some points that the traditions in question have in common.

The common denominator for fields 1 and 3 is that both are defined by the fact that the traditions in question seek the source of social problems in the social structure of society. On the one side, we have Saint-Simon and the whole of the succeeding and powerful tradition, that is, positivist social science. Björn Eriksson has characterised this tradition as 'sociology as agent activity' (see chapter 2). In other words, there is a theory about society (and social problems), a programme for the work of social change, and a group of people who see themselves as agents of change. The historical tradition brought out in field 1 also formulates a fundamental attitude to which social work as a scientific discipline lays claim. This fundamental attitude, or basic assumption, comprises a whole, consisting in theory, programme and agents of change. On the other side (field 3), we have a group of agents of change, Jane Addams and her colleagues at the Hull House Settlement, who, on the basis of their practical social work, develop working methods and knowledge that are intertwined, or which can compete with the approaches of, for example, the Chicago School of Sociology. In the zone where these two areas of characteristics meet, two traditions also meet, both of which are of considerable interest to the discipline of social work.

We have seen that the Saint-Simonist tradition forms an obvious background of ideas to the subject of sociology, particularly its positivist tradition. In chapter 3, I argued that the same tradition in the history of ideas can, and should be, acknowledged by the discipline of social work. The reasons I gave for this are, on the one hand, the fundamental structure of social work, in which theory and the work of social change are included as explicit elements, and on the other, the fundamental interest of social work in knowledge, which is an emancipatory interest, aimed at using knowledge to make life better for mankind and to help people at risk. In chapter 6, we have studied Jane Addams's practical work and her contribution to the building-up of knowledge in social work. Addams and her settlement tradition form an obvious background of ideas to the subject of social work. But just as obviously, Mary Jo Deegan argues in favour of designating Jane Addams as the greatest sociologist of her time. These two examples show how the history-of-ideas boundaries between areas of characteristics 1 and 3 can be erased, and that two disciplines can lay claim to the same traditions in the history of ideas.

In a corresponding way, we can now consider the relationship between fields of characteristics 2 and 4. As we know, the common denominator is that the traditions in question focus on the individual as the source of social problems. The difference between these traditions is that the one begins with theory and then proceeds to practice, while the other starts with practice and goes over to theory. Mary Richmond, who launched and developed the social casework method, because of her practical achievements and theoretical approaches, belongs to the discipline of social work. On the other hand, we have also seen how influences from field 2 assert themselves when it comes to the later development of the social casework method. The discipline of psychology asserts itself strongly in relation to social casework by force of its being the main supplier of theories necessary to the development of the casework method. It is not until much later that social work starts trying to free itself from the grip of psychology. It is also more recently that psychosocial work, the heir to casework, creates a distinctive image of its own in relation to psychotherapy, for example. From chapters 4 and 5, we can draw the conclusion that the boundary between fields of characteristics 2 and 4 is rather fluid, and that the disciplines of social work and psychology lay claim to the working field that lies in the borderland.

But what about the boundaries between the fields of characteristics that are horizontal to each other? The common denominator in the upper half of the four-field table is the history-of-ideas tendency 'from theory to practice', while the difference lies in whether it is society or the individual in focus as the main source of social problems. The common denominator implies that research results and theoretical knowledge form the base for the work of social change. This does not mean, which was also pointed out in chapter 2, that the role of practice is minimised in the interplay between theory and practice just because theory holds a prominent place in this connection. The object under study is first defined theoretically and is then given a more-operational definition. The practical application, or the work of social change, depends on the theoretical point of departure. The theoretical orientation in question here means that there is a tendency to delimit the object of study, and thereby also what is to be the object of the work of social change. It has been particularly attractive in terms of 'society' and 'the individual', but also later in terms of macro, meso, and micro as designations of different levels of analysis and action – a terminology that indicates the view of the complexity of social problems, but also an indication of the division of work between different disciplines. It has not been my intention to discuss this complex of problems within the framework of Saint-Simon's thinking or to discuss casework from the standpoint of psychological approaches. The question of division of work, however, has been explicitly discussed by Berglind (see chapter 2).

The lower half of the four-field table has as its common definition that the fields are characterised by the history-of-ideas tendency 'from practice to theory', while the difference lies in whether we seek the source of social problems in society or in the individual. The base for social change is practical activity itself. From the history-of-ideas perspective, pioneers have tended to choose either society or the individual as their main areas of work. Those who work in the field and who come into contact with the complexity of social problems find out sooner or later the interplay and importance of the various levels of problems. This is, of course, also true of the pioneers presented in this book. Mary Richmond's point of departure was that the causes of social problems were mainly to be sought in the individual. She realised, however, that the work of social change should also be directed towards society, with the result that causes of social problems should be sought in society. This is clearly shown in Richmond's diagram 'The rhythm of social work', where the term 'mass betterment' stands for the work of social change directed at society. This is an opinion that Richmond suppressed in her controversy with Jane Addams. Addams considered the work of social change oriented towards the individual to be system-preserving, and she recommended social work that attacks social problems at a structural level. There was, however, also a doubleness in Addams, and it revealed itself in the working methods developed and applied at Hull House. One of the most important working areas was direct social service, and this meant that they worked with a wide range of social problems as they manifested themselves among the inhabitants of the district. There was, in other words, an awareness, based on practical activity, of the complicated character of social problems.

One dimension of the history of ideas that is built into the theoretical frame of reference of the study, and which has been carved out at various phases of the inquiry, is that the field of knowledge defined by the four-field table has become the object of a process of specialisation. This has meant that, in the field of knowledge, areas of interest have been established which different disciplines lay claim to. Each discipline claims that a certain area of knowledge belongs to just that discipline, and they do this by force of having developed theories and methodological instruments to work on the area of knowledge, and by reinforcing these efforts with institutionalised means, such as organisation, monopoly in awarding degrees, and so on. For natural reasons, there arises tension now and then between different disciplines in questions concerning common fields of knowledge. This book provides a background in the history of ideas to how disciplines such as sociology, psychology, and social work move and interact within areas of knowledge that can be regarded as common to them all. Relationships with disciplines such as, for example, social policy, social law, psychiatry, and social medicine have not been explicitly discussed. But my survey of the history of ideas shows the importance of studies in the history of ideas as a background to an assessment of disciplines' boundaries, objects of study, questions at issue, theory areas, and so on. In brief, insights into the history of ideas are central to the understanding, recognition and legitimisation of the *raison d'être* of disciplines as fields of knowledge or research disciplines.

History of ideas and fields of knowledge

Brante (1987) states various legitimisation strategies for new fields of research or knowledge. These strategies can be of cognitive or social character. Cognitive legitimisation strategies can claim that a new field of knowledge is required because (a) there is a lack of knowledge within a special area of reality; (b) it is possible to delimit a new field of knowledge in relation to the already established disciplines in that area, or (c) it is possible to state the subject matter of the new field of knowledge. The social legitimisation of the discipline is performed by stating the practical usefulness of the new field of knowledge.

Brante, who studies the establishment of social work as an independent scientific discipline in Sweden, describes the development of the history of ideas in an already established discipline, namely sociology, in order to provide pedagogical examples of how the legitimisation process of that discipline came about. Brante, like many others before him, establishes that 'the classics of sociology, naturally enough, went to great pains to find meta-ideas, that is to carve out what was specific to their discipline'.

The same type of attempts are being made in modern times in Sweden to define the field of knowledge of social work, and thereby also legitimise the discipline of social work (see Swedner 1983, Börjeson 1984, Berglind 1983, Nygren 1992). Brante (1987) himself interviewed the then professors of social work in order to illustrate similarities and differences in their perceptions of the discipline of social work. The following opinions emerged from Brante's study:

'Professor 1: One possible way of defining research in social work is to say that we are interested in knowing in what way we can intervene in the social systems in order to overcome problems. These interventions can lie on the micro-level, the meso-level or the macro-level.

'Professor 2: The discipline is engaged in the study of social problems at different levels, the macro-, micro- and meso-levels. We should, then, pay attention to both the causes of the problems and measures to counter them.

'Professor 3: If one were to support these practitioner-oriented claims, one would be doing the whole thing a disservice, because it would mean that many of the approaches to the problems would be very narrow, arranged, consensus-stamped and so on. Social work will never be a discipline like sociology. I'm damned if I know what will become of it.

'Professor 4: Research in the discipline of social work must essentially be research that deals with what different interested parties call social work. That is to say, it is not my intention to say what it should be like or anything like that, but to say what one does in social work.

'What I am personally interested in is opportunities for reflection. What it is that people do when they say they can do something and know

something and say what they will do with other people? There is a need
for reflection upon these social engineering strategies.'

Brante's conclusion is that social work stands out as a subject of knowledge
without its own object of knowledge. A new discipline that develops on
account of specialisation or new discoveries already has a basic puzzle, around
which researchers can gather to develop a cumulative research tradition, he
thinks. In the case of social work, such basic requirements are lacking (Brante
1987).

'The four professors give different suggestions for possible conceptual
frameworks to start from. One proposal was the concept "interven-
tion", linked to the concept of "field of meaning"; another was the
discrepancy between the actual and ideal situation; a third was "people-
processing organisations", and the fourth was to discontinue the
discipline as it is, after all, not possible to create such a science. The
first three proposals, however, provide the most form, and have less to
say concerning content.

They do not succeed in stating the unique puzzle that could motivate
the new field of research' (emphasis added).

A new attempt to narrow down the field of knowledge of the discipline has
been made by Lennart Nygren (1992). According to Nygren, social work as a
scientific discipline involves 'seeking knowledge about what it means in some
form of organisation to work in the direction of change with people in socially
vulnerable life situations'. Nygren develops a so-called cartography to narrow
down the field of knowledge of the discipline. The cartography most resembles
a three-dimensional area of characteristics, with the variables 'levels of
knowledge', 'actors' fields' and 'time aspects'. The levels of knowledge
concept, which is borrowed from Börjeson (1984), aims at stating the capacity
of the knowledge to explain and understand, and its 'depth'. The concept
comprises four levels: (a) transcendent knowledge with the scope to go beyond
its own area of knowledge; (b) knowledge with a theoretical depth of intention
which works from theoretical conceptual frameworks and is provocative
towards established concepts; (c) applied research, meaning the acceptance of
established theoretical frameworks and testing these against different aspects
of reality; (d) practice as knowledge, meaning the utilisation of human action,
a sort of claims that 'one must research and plan knowledge projects at a level
not lower than (b) . . . if one is to be able to justifiably claim an independent area
of knowledge'.

Nygren outlines, in a programmatic manner, a number of actors' fields which he sees as interest areas of social work. The most central actors' field consists in the meeting between fellow human being (client) and social worker, when the work of social change is carried on. The meeting is assumed to provide a basic dimension in social work. Social work is always carried on within the framework of a given organisation, and this is why organisations for the work of change are the other actors' field of importance to the field of knowledge of social work. Nygren gives social policy as the third actors' field, as this defines opportunities and limitations for social work. The fourth actors' field consists in studies of oppression and exclusion mechanisms. The fifth and final actors' field is the global context, which refers to the internationalisation of the economy, culture, and the dissemination of knowledge.

Only a rather brief description is given of the third dimension, but, as far as I can understand, its aim is process thinking. Nygren writes that 'social work is carried out with people who are involved in a process of development'. There are, therefore, different stages in all the actors' fields described.

FIGURE 7.2   The field of knowledge in social work
Source: Nygren 1992

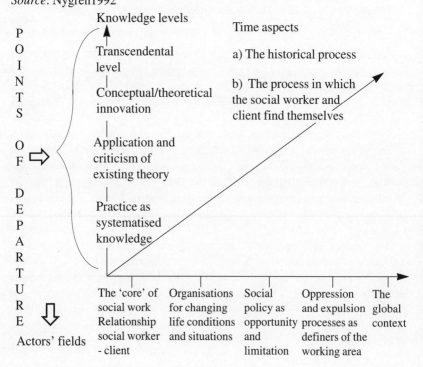

From the diagram, it can be seen that Nygren's cartography narrows down a field of knowledge that the discipline of social work can lay claim to. In comparison with earlier attempts to define the field of knowledge of the discipline, Nygren's approach is the most far-reaching. There is a certain similarity between Nygren's and Berglind's (see chapter 2) approaches – both of them have as their ambition to bring out a picture of the whole for studies of what are considered to be social problems, and wish to bring about change to improve people's conditions of life. But there are also differences between these approaches. One of essentiality that is relevant to the argument here is that Berglind recommends a more 'traditional' division of work between a number of disciplines, including social work. It is proposed that different disciplines supply knowledge on different parts of a certain complex of problems by making use of different fields of knowledge. Nygren adopts an expansionist attitude and sees possible areas for social work in a composite and complicated conglomerate of actors' fields. Social work is given a wide role in a comprehensive field of knowledge.

Nygren, like many others before him, draws a programmatic outline to narrow down the field of knowledge of social work. I see this as being normal and correct for a discipline that wishes to lay claim to its own field of knowledge. But the issue that Nygren does not discuss, and which meets with opposition when Brante so clearly formulates it, is how this field of knowledge is to be legitimised.

I can very well imagine that a discipline like social psychology, which has been reactivated during the 1980s, can lay claim to including the actors' field 'meeting' in its field of knowledge. The actors' field 'organisations for the changing of living conditions and life situation' can be studied within sociology or business administration. Social policy as a discipline lays traditional claim to assuming just 'social policy as opportunity and limitation' as its field of knowledge. The actors' field 'oppression and exclusion processes' is a traditional field of knowledge for sociology. 'The global context' is studied by several disciplines, among others political science and comparative social policy. The above mentioned, as well as other disciplines, often have a more sophisticated battery of theories and methodological achievements. In that situation, the question of the legitimisation of the new field of knowledge of social work is of vital importance.

It is my opinion that it is right that a discipline like social work should seek to establish a field of knowledge of its own by being normative and programmatic. In this respect, social work is no exception in the social and behavioural sciences. I also think that the legitimisation of the new field of knowledge is an empirical question, in the sense that the success of the discipline in legitimising itself is dependent on a number of phenomena. Let me indicate some points that I believe to be of central importance.

- In the cartography presented by Nygren, there is an *integrating* element. By this I mean that the cartography outlines and argues in favour of a set of actors' fields, where the understanding of the mutual relationships of the fields is a question of its own. We are dealing with a whole. The whole cannot be reduced to the sum of its parts. This point of departure, the integrative element, in the field of knowledge presupposes that a methodology is developed to handle problems like these. Can we, for example, integrate the actors' field 'meeting' into the other actors' fields? Can we demonstrate relationships between some or all of these actors' fields which we have so far not foreseen? Are there other actors' fields of vital importance? If social work can succeed in this task, this will, in my opinion, be a base for legitimising the new field of knowledge.

- I share the opinion of Börjeson and Nygren that a field of research with a legitimised base of its own must be able to work with knowledge levels designated as transcendent "knowledge", or as knowledge with a theoretical depth of intention. The latter level, knowledge with a theoretical depth of intention, knowledge that critically examines and reflects upon its own battery of theories, is a minimum. The knowledge level requirement also presupposes that the subject develops a new methodological front line of its own. If this is successful, the subject should have a base for legitimising the new field of knowledge.

- In the way the new field of knowledge is narrowed down in the cartography, it includes an element that can be called the action aspect of social work, or the work of social change. The action aspect is an integral part of the cartography. This is an explicit element, and there is no other discipline that expresses it in such a clear way. The action aspect can be found, for example, in certain types of sociology, but not in the whole of sociology as a discipline. Here the new field of knowledge has a unique opportunity to develop a base for legitimisation. I am not only thinking of social legitimisation, which is obvious, but of a cognitive legitimisation built on knowledge of the action aspect.

- Programmatic cartographies need all the support they can get, especially in a longer perspective. It is important that a new discipline is driven forward by both intrascientific criteria and extrascientific demands. A positive development tendency for a new discipline, a new field of knowledge, is obviously better than a negative one for the legitimisation process of the discipline in the somewhat longer term. In this respect, a tried and tested instrument is how well established disciplines are in the context of the history of their ideas. If it can be claimed that an approach like Nygren's is not an ahistorical construction, but that it can, on the contrary, be traced in a history of ideas context (especially in the emergence of social science), this will be of decisive importance to the development of an identity.

It is the well-known predicament of social work that forms the basis of the article in which Nygren (1992:46) develops his cartography:

'I think that social work in a broad sense has always been defined as either different practitioners (fields in which different professional groups work) or as fields of knowledge. In the latter case, it has often been taken for granted that social work is interdisciplinary, and – at least within the education system – social work has often been described as the sum of knowledge in something else: psychology, political science, sociology and so on. It is therefore my opinion that the way of thinking that lies behind the establishment of social work as a "subject" or "discipline" means a one-sided emphasis of what "social workers generally do", or – in Sweden in any case – "what a degree course at a School of Social Work traditionally contains"' (emphasis original).

We can rightly ask ourselves why things have developed this way, and there are very probably several reasons for it. From the viewpoint of this book, some aspects are worth noting. That social work has been defined as different practitioners is easy to understand. Social work has rich and obvious roots in its professional development. This professional development has taken place within the framework of the history-of-ideas tendency 'from practice to theory'. If you go through historical descriptions of social work, you can also see that they take professional development, with its organisational and ethical questions in the foreground, as their starting point. Therefore, they have been one-sidedly oriented towards the history-of-ideas tendency 'from practice to theory', and have been unable to integrate other development tendencies as these have manifested themselves in the arena of ideas. It is also, then, easier to understand that, when defining social work as a field of knowledge, this definition has been reduced to 'the sum of knowledge in something else', since efforts have not been made to find a place for social work within the framework of the 'from theory to have been observed that it would have been possible to establish the subject in traditions in the history of ideas; these could then form the embryo of identity-providing and identity-developing processes.

Instead of a conclusion
It lies in the nature of an approach to problems that a study of this kind generates more questions than it is able to answer. Some of the issues in this book were the point of departure for the study, others have arisen as the study proceeded. Certain matters have been discussed, others have been hinted at. In conclusion, I shall mention, and to some extent recapitulate, some of the questions at issue that stand out as being important from the viewpoint of the state of knowledge in the discipline and the legitimacy crisis that social work finds itself in.

- From a history-of-ideas perspective, there is a large area of issues that includes, among other things, the terms 'social problem', 'people at risk', poor classes' and 'the needy'. The number of terms can be increased and varied, but most concepts, nevertheless, revolve around ideas whose content is covered by the terms above. On the basis of an interest in knowing how *to understand, to explain, and to do something about* social and human siuations, a tradition has developed in the history of ideas. This tradition has its roots in the origins and development of social science. The most prominent elements of the tradition comprise the idea of theories about social and human conditions, the idea of a programme that can form the basis of the work of social change, and the idea of the need for a group of people to become involved in the work of change. The empirical survey undertaken in the book shows that the set of ideas in social work is to be sought in these domains. We can perhaps also assume that it is in these domains that we shall search for the core of social work.

- It becomes apparent that there are several disciplines that lay claim to being specific sets of ideas belonging to these domains. These disciplines try out similar conceptual constructions to handle the issues in question; more often, they are the source of more-sophisticated sets of concepts. They have more to say about the issues of interest. They also seem to have stronger self-esteem as disciplines and a greater degree of legitimacy; this is a consequence of their inner scientific consistency and better self-insight, thanks to their being more firmly established in a historical context of ideas. There is, however, one problem left to investigate: these disciplines, in contrast to social work, do not seem necessarily to consider that their respective cores belong to those domains indicated above as belonging to social work. Neighbouring disciplines have other conceptual fields which they regard as specific and central. Such a delimitation of sets of ideas, which up to now have been largely hidden, opens up new opportunities for the discipline of social work. I consider this to be a possible and important area of research.

- Establishing the boundaries of a discipline and identifying its core can be done in various ways. As I said in Chapter 1, we can look at what the discipline actually studies, or allocate a specific factual area to the discipline, or exposewhat the discipline has achieved. If we choose to study what the discipline has achieved we are in historical territory, where the tradition of the discipline as set of ideas is brought into focus. For me, it is necessary for a discipline like social work to be the object of thorough surveys into the history of its ideas. Perspectives on 'what has the discipline achieved?' also mean new perspectives on 'what is the discipline doing?' and 'what is the discipline to do?' It is my conviction that perspectives on the history of the discipline's ideas are identity-forming, and this will in all probability influence the legitimacy of it.

- Narrowing down the history of ideas in a discipline like social work is no easy task. In all probability the task requires working on conceptual apparatuses that go beyond conventional working methods. In surveys of histories of ideas presented so far, three types of approach have been chosen. One way is to construct the survey around the thinkers themselves. In thisway, sets of ideas have been revealed by looking at the achievements of the thinkers chosen. An example of this type of approach is, for instance, Sven-Erik Liedman's works on Swedish intellectuals (Liedman 1986,1991). The second way of working involves studying the historical ideas content of various schools that have been formed. The focus of interest here is on charting the premises, ideas and theories in systems of thought in the way they are summarised within the framework of a specific school. One example of this is Tom Bottomore's and Robert Nisbet's *A History of Sociological Analysis* (1978). A third way of approaching the history of ideas is to adopt the method of the American philosopher Arthur Lovejoy. In his lectures at Harvard in 1933, Lovejoy put forward the idea that the history of ideas should study composites, or elements in thought systems, which he called 'unit-ideas'. These unit-ideas are, above all, 'implicit or incompletely explicit *assumptions*, or more or *less unconscious mental habits*, operating in the thought of an individual or a generation' (Lovejoy 1964). They are often of a very general character, but their aim is to narrow down the most central elements in a set of ideas. Research on social work should not hesitate to act on a wide front by using the good ideas to be found in the various approaches.

- In the previous sections, I noted that social work must aim at trying out levels of knowledge that are designated transcendent, and that possessing a theoretical depth of intention. This means critically examining its own conceptual field and, hopefully, breaking through the given traditional limits. I have previously mentioned the term 'social problem'. Transcendent knowledge would, for example, analyse this concept in a revolutionary way, and with marked consequences for practice. What is a social problem? Is it an ahistorical concept? Or is it a social construction which takes on different shapes and meanings in different historical situations? What do theoretical insights that can be provided by means of transcendent knowledge mean for the concept 'social problem' which social work engages with today? Insights into the history of its ideas can do nothing but make considerable contributions towards orienting the discipline in the direction of more-sophisticated levels of knowledge.

- Social work as a degree subject provides a frame for social work as a research discipline. The frame consists, among other things, in the fact that there are students and researchers of the subject. Those who represent the academic discipline are also the agents who will be able to develop the identity of the discipline and contribute to its legitimisation. Students of the discipline must devote themselves to studies of its roots in the history of its ideas to a far greater extent than is the case today.

Bibliography

Abrahamsson, B and Broström, A (1979) *Om arbetets rätt. Vägar till ekonomisk demokrati* Stockholm, Almqvist & Wiksell

Addams, J (1895) 'Prefatory Note', 'The Settlement as a Factor in the Labor Movement' in Residents of Hull House *Hull House Maps and Papers. A Presentation of Nationalities and Wages in a Congested District of Chicago, Together with Comments and Essays on Problems Growing out of the Social Conditions* New York, Thomas Y Crowell, ppvii-viii, 183-204.

Addams, J (1896) 'A Belated Industry' *American Journal of Sociology* 1(March) pp536-50.

Addams, J (1902) *Democracy and Social Ethics* ed Anne Firor Scott, Cambridge, Mass, Harvard University Press 1964.

Addams, J (1905) 'Problems of Municipal Administration' *American Journal of Sociology* 10(January), pp425-44

Addams, J (1907) *Newer Ideals of Peace* New York, Macmillan

Addams, J (1908) 'Comment on an article by John R Commons' *American Journal of Sociology* 13(May), pp770-73.

Addams, J (1909) *The Spirit of Youth and the City Streets* New York, Macmillan

Addams, J (1910) *Twenty Years at Hull House* New York, Macmillan

Addams, J (1912) 'Recreation as a Public Function in Urban Communities' *American Journal of Sociology* 17(March), pp615-19.

Addams, J (1914) 'A Modern Devil-Baby' *American Journal of Sociology* 20(July), pp117-18.

Addams, J (1922) *Peace and Bread in Time of War* Boston, Hall

Addams, J (1930) *The Second Twenty Years at Hull House* New York, Macmillan

Addams, J (1932) *My Friend, Julia Lathrop* New York, Macmillan

Addams, J (1960) *A Centennial Reader* ed Emily Cooper Johnson, New York, Macmillan

Allardt, E (1965) *Samhällsstruktur och sociala spänningar* Tammerfors, Söderströms

Allardt, E, Lysgaard, S and Bøttger Sørensen, A (1988) *Sociologin i Sverige. Vetenskap, miljö och organisation* Stockholm, HSFR/UHÄ

Almqvist, M (1969) *Inledning till socialvårdsmetodik* Lund, Studentlitteratur

Aron, R (1965) *Main Currents in Sociological Thought 1* Middlesex, Penguin Books, 1968

Asplund, J (1987) *Det sociala livets elemetära former* Göteborg, Korpen

Baker-Benfield, G J (1979) 'Mother Emancipator: The Meaning of Jane Addams' Sickness and Cure' *Journal of Family History* 4(4), pp395-420

Becker, D (1964) 'Exit Lady Bountiful' *Social Service Review* 38(1), pp57-72

Beckman, S (1985) *Kärlek på tjänstetid. Om amatörer och professionella inom vården* Stockholm, Arbetslivscentrum

Berglind, H (1983) 'Sociala problem och socialt arbete. Om praxis och forskning i socialt arbete' *Sociologisk Forskning* 2, pp16-29

Bernal, D J (1954) *Science in History*, vol IV Harmondsworth, Pelican Books, 1965

Bernler, G and Johnsson, L (1985) *Handledning i psykosocialt arbete* Stockholm, Natur och Kultur

Bernler, G and Johnsson, L (1988) *Teori för psykosocialt arbete* Stockholm. Natur och Kultur

Bernler, G and Johnsson, L (1989) *Att handleda praktikanter i sociala yrken* Stockholm, Natur och Kultur

Blalock, H M (1961) *Causal Inferences in Nonexperimental Research* Chapel Hill, The University of Northern Carolina Press

Boehm, W W (1958) 'The nature of social work' *Social Work* 3(2), pp10-18

Börjeson, B (1984) *Om socialt arbete som ett kunskapsområde* Umeå universitet, Institution för socialt arbete, rapport 24

Bottomore, T and Nisbet, R (eds) (1978) *A History of Sociological Analysis* London, Heinemann

Bowers, S (1949) 'Nature and definition of social case work' *Journal of Social Case Work* 30(8), pp311-17

Brante, T (1987) 'Om konstitueringen av nya vetenskapliga fält – exemplet forskning om socialt arbete' *Sociologisk forskning* 4, pp30-60

Brieland, D (1990) 'The Hull House Tradition and the Contemporary Social Worker: Was Jane Addams Really a Social Worker?' *Social Work* 35(2), pp134-38

Broadhurst, B (1971) *Social Thought, Social Practice, and Social Work Education – Sanborn, Ely, Warner, Richmond* New York, Columbia University (PhD thesis, University Microfilms International)

Bruno, F J (1948) *Trends in Social Work as Reflected in the Proceedings of the National Conference of Social Work 1874-1946* New York, Columbia University Press

Bulmer, M (1984) *The Chicago School of Sociology* Chicago, University of Chicago Press

Bulmer, M (1989) 'Jane Addams and the Men of the Chicago School, 1892-1918' *American Journal of Sociology* 94(6), pp1479-81

Chambers, C A (1963) *Seedtime of Reform: American Social Service and Social Action 1918-1933* Minneapolis, University of Minnesota Press

Charléty, S (1931) *Histoire du Saint-Simonisme* Paris, Gonthier

Conway, J (1964) 'Jane Addams: An American Heroine' in Lifton, R J (ed) *The Women in America* Boston, Beacon Press, 1967, pp247-66

Cook, B W (1989) 'The Impact of Anti-Communism in American Life' *Science & Society* 53(4), pp470-75

Davis, A F (1967) *Spearheads for Reform. The Social Settlement and theProgressive Movement 1890-1914* London, Oxford University Press, 1970

de Condorcet, M J (1795) *Esquisse d'un tableau historique des progrés de l'esprit humain* New York, Georg Olms Verlag, 1981

Deegan, M J (1978) 'Women in Sociology, 1890-1930' *Journal of the History of Sociology 1* (Fall), pp11-34

Deegan, M J (1981) 'Early Women Sociologists and the American Sociological Society: The Patterns of Exclusion and Participation' *The American Sociologist* 16 (February), pp14-24

Deegan, M J (1988a) 'W E B. Du Bois and the Women of Hull House,1895-1899' *The American Sociologist* 19(14), pp301-11

Deegan, M J (1988b) *Jane Addams and the Men of the Chicago School 1892-1918* New Brunswick, Transaction Books, 1990 de Schweinitz, K (1924) *The Art of Helping People out of Trouble* New York, Houghton Mifflin

Durkheim, E (1928) *Socialism and Saint-Simon* London, Routledge & Kegan Paul, 1959

Durkheim, E (1953) *Sociology and Philosophy* Glencoe, The Free Press

Egidius, H (ed) (1978) *Psykosocialt arbetssätt* Stockholm, Natur och Kultur

Elias, N (1939) *Sedernas Historia* Stockholm, Atlantis, 1989

Eliasson, R (1987) *Forskningsetik och perspektivval* Lund, Studentlitteratur

Ellenhorn, R (1988) 'Toward a Humanistic Social Work: Social Work for Conviviality' *Humanity & Society* 12(2), pp166-88

Elson, A (1954) 'First Principles of Jane Addams' *Social Service Review* 28(March), pp3-11

Eriksson, B (1981) 'Om sociologin och paradigm' *Sociologisk Forskning* 1, pp3-17

Eriksson, B (1988) *Samhällsvetenskapens uppkomst. En tolkning ur den sociologiska traditionens perspektiv* Uppsala, Hallgren & Fallgren

Fish, V K (1985) 'Hull House: Pioneer in Urban Research During its Creative Years' *History of Sociology* 6(1), pp33-54

Fourier, C (1836-37) *Slaget om de små pastejerna* Stockholm, Federativ, 1983

Frängsmyr, T (1980) *Framsteg eller förfall. Framtidsbilder och utopier i västerländsk tanketradition* Stockholm, Liber

Franklin, D L (1986) 'Mary Richmond and Jane Addams: From Moral Certainty to Rational Inquiry in Social Work Practice' *Social Service Review* 60(4), pp504-25

Gartland, R (1940) 'Editorial notes' *The Family* 21(4), pp125-6

Germain, C B and Gitterman, A (1980) *The Life Model of Social Work Practice* New York, Columbia University Press

Germain, C B and Hartman, A (1980) 'People and Ideas in the History of Social Work Practice' Social Casework. *The Journal of Contemporary Social Work* (June), pp323-31

Gitterman, A and Germain, C B (1976) 'Social work practice: A life model' *Social Service Review* 50(4), pp601-10

Goetschius, G (1969) *Working with Community Groups* London, Routledge & Kegan Paul

Gouldner, A (1961) 'Anti-minotaur: The myth of a value-free sociology' in Horowitz, I L (ed.) *The New Sociology* New York, Oxford University Press, 1964, pp196-217

Gouldner, A (1973) For Sociology. Renewal and Critique in *Sociology Today* Middlesex, Penguin Books

Greenstone, D J (1979) 'Dorothea Dix and Jane Addams: From Transcendentalism to Pragmatism in American Social Reform' *Social Service Review* 53(4), pp527-59

Hatje, A-K (1974) *Befolkningsfrågan och välfärden. Debatten om familjepolitik och nativitetsökning under 1930- och 1940-talen* Stockholm, Allmänna Förlaget

Healy, W (1915) *The Individual Delinquent* Boston, Little, Brown & Co.

Hessle, S (1982) *Att arbeta med människor. Riktlinjer för psykosocialt arbete* Stockholm, AWE/GEBERS

Hirdman, Y (1989) *Att lägga livet till rätta. Studier i svensk folkhemspolitik* Stockholm, Carlssons

Hollis, F (1964) *Casework: A Psychological Therapy* New York, Random House

Hollis, F and Woods, M (1981) *Casework: A Psychosocial Therapy* New York, Random House

Holmberg, P (1978) *Socialpolitik i teori och praktik* Stockholm, Prisma

Hull-House Maps and Papers. A Presentation of Nationalities and Wages in a Congested District of Chicago, Together with Comments and Essays on Problems Growing out of the Social Conditions (1895), by Residents of Hull House, New York, Thomas Y Crowell & Co

Ideal och verkligheter i svensk socialvård (1976), Berglind, H (ed), Stockholm, Wahlström & Widstrand

Kahn, A (ed) (1959) *Issues in American Social Work* New York, Columbia University Press

Kälvemark, A-S (1980) *More Children of Better Quality? Aspects of Swedish Population Policy in the 1930s* Uppsala, Almqvist & Wiksell International

Kelley, F (1895) 'The Sweating-System' *Hull-House Maps and Papers* (see above), pp27-45

Lasch, C (ed.) (1965) *The Social Thought of Jane Addams* Indianapolis, Bobbs-Merrill

Leiby, J (1978) *History of Social Welfare and Social Work in the United States* New York, Columbia University Press

Lengerman, P M (1989) 'Jane Addams and the Men of the Chicago School,1892-1918' *Contemporary Sociology* 18(4), pp599-600

Lennéer-Axelson, B and Thylefors, I (1982) *Psykosocialt behandlingsarbete* Stockholm, Natur och Kultur

Levine, D (1971) *Jane Addams and the Liberal Tradition* Maddison, State Historical Society of Wisconsin

Liedman, S-E (1973) 'Marxism och idéhistoria. En skiss' in Norén, K (ed) *Människans samhälleliga vara. Marxistisk forskningsteori i humanistisk forskning* Kristianstad, Cavefors Bokförlag

Liedman, S-E (1977) *Motsatsernas spel* Lund, Cavefors Bokförlag

Liedman, S-E (1983) *Arbetsfördelning, självmord och nytta* Örebro, Högskolan i Örebro, Skriftserie

Liedman, S-E (1986) *Den synliga handen* Stockholm, Arbetarkultur

Liedman, S-E (1991) *Att förändra världen – men med måtta* Stockholm, Arbetarkultur

Lindholm, S (1979) *Vetenskap, verklighet och paradigm* Stockholm, AWE/GEBERS

Linn, J W (1935) *Jane Addams: A Biography* New York, D Appleton-Century

Lovejoy, A O (1936) *The Great Chain of Being. A Study of the History of an Idea* Cambridge, Mass, Harvard University Press

Lowry, F (1937) 'Objectives in Social Casework' *The Family* 18(8), pp261-68

Månsson, S-A (1990) 'Den kvalitativa sociologin och det sociala arbetet' in Goldberg, T (ed) *Den ömsesidiga utmaningen* Stockholm, Gothia, pp15-41

Manuel, F E (1956) *The New World of Henri Saint-Simon* Cambridge, Mass, Harvard University Press

Markham, F M H (1952) *Henri, Comte de Saint-Simon: Selected Writings* London, Basil Blackwell

Mead, G H (1934) *Mind, Self and Society* Chicago, The University of Chicago Press

Myrdal, G (1967) *Objectivity in Social Research* New York, Pantheon Books, 1969

Myrdal, G and Myrdal, A (1934) *Kris i befolkningsfrågan* Stockholm, Bonniers

Nedeljkovic, Y-R (1989) 'Historical Bases of Social Work Science and Practice', ERG-seminar, Bled, Yugoslavia

Nilsson, K and Sunesson, S (1988) *Konflikt, kontroll, expertis* Lund, Arkiv

Nisbeth, R (1980) *History of the Idea of Progress* London, Heinemann

Nygren, L (1992) 'Socialt arbete – ett kunskapsområde i förändring' *Nordisk Sosial Arbeid* 1, pp45-59

Oeuvres choisies de C H Saint-Simon (1859), published by C Lemonnier, Brussels, van Meenen

Oeuvres complètes de Saint-Simon (1932) Paris, Naquet

Oeuvres de Saint-Simon (1941), published by O Rodrigues, Paris, Capella

Oeuvres de Saint-Simon et d'Enfantin (1865-1878) Paris, Dentu 1865-1876, Paris, Leroux 1877-1878

Parsons, T (1951) *The Social System* London, Routledge & Kegan Paul, 1970

Perlman, H H (1965) 'Case work and the diminished man' in Lurie, N V (ed) *Encyclopedia of Social Work* New York, National Association of Social Workers

Popper, K R (1957) *The Poverty of Historicism* London, Routledge & Kegan Paul, 1969

Popper, K R (1959) *The Logic of Scientific Discovery* London, Hutchinson

Popper, K R (1972) *Objective Knowledge. An Evolutionary Approach* Oxford, The Clarendon Press, 1974

Pottick, K J (1989) 'Jane Addams Revisited: Practice Theory and Social Economics' *Social Work with Groups* 11(4), pp11-26

Pumphrey, M W (1956) *Mary Richmond and the Rise of Professional Social Work in Baltimore: The Foundations of a Creative Career* New York, Columbia University (PhD thesis, University Microfilms International)

Pumphrey, M W (1957) "The first step" – Mary Richmond's earliest professional reading 1889-91' *Social Service Review* XXXI (June), pp144-63

Richmond, M (1899) *Friendly Visiting Among the Poor. A Handbook for Charity Workers* New York, Macmillan

Richmond, M (1915) 'The social case worker in a changing world' *Proceedings of the National Conference of Charities and Corrections* Chicago, National Conference of Charities and Corrections

Richmond, M (1917) *Social Diagnosis* New York, Russell Sage Foundation

Richmond, M (1922) *What is Social Case Work? An Introductory Description* New York, Russell Sage Foundation

Richmond, M (1930) *The Long View. Papers and Addresses* Colcord, J C (ed), New York, Russell Sage Foundation

Roberts, R W and Nee, R H (eds) (1970) *Theories of Social Casework* Chicago, University of Chicago Press

Robinson, V (1930) *A Changing Psychology in Social Casework* Philadelphia, University of Pennsylvania Press

Robinson, V (ed) (1962) Jessie Taft. *Therapist and Social Work Educator: A Professional Biography* Philadelphia, University of Pennsylvania Press

Ronnby, A (1981) *Socialstaten. Till kritiken av socialteknokratin* Lund, Studentlitteratur

Ronnby, A (1983) *Socialarbetets förklaringsmodeller* Stockholm, Liber

Ross, E A (1910) *Social Control* New York, Macmillan

Rothman, J (1974) *Planning and Organizing for Social Change* New York, Columbia University Press

Rubington, E and Weinberg, M S (1971) *The Study of Social Problems. Five Perspectives* London, Oxford University Press

Salomon, A (1955) *The Tyranny of Progress. Reflections on the Origins of Sociology* New York, The Noonday Press

Shalin, D N (1990) 'Jane Addams and the Men of the Chicago School, 1892-1918' *Theory and Society* 19(1), pp127-32

Smalley, R E (1970) 'The Functional Approach to Casework Practice' in Roberts, R W and Nee, R H (eds) *Theories of Social Casework* Chicago, University of Chicago Press

SOU 1974:39 *Socialvården. Mål och medel* (Principbetänkande av socialutredningen)

SOU 1977:40 *Socialtjänst och socialförsäkringstillägg. Lagar och motiv* (Socialutredningens slutbetänkande)

Sundh, K and Turunen, P (eds) (1992) *Social mobilisering. Om samhällsarbete i Sverige* Stockholm, Publica

Swedner, G and Swedner, H (1990) 'Jane Addams. Socialarbetare och fredsarbetare' *Socionomen* 3, pp18-23

Swedner, H (1983) *Socialt arbete. En tankeram* Lund, Liber

Swedner, H (1985) *Forskning i socialt arbete. Dess historiska bakgrund och utvecklingsmöjligheter* Göteborg, Skrifter om socialt arbete nr 1, Institutionen för socialt arbete, Göteborgs universitet

Swedner, H (1987) *Etik och kongruens i välfärdsarbetet* Göteborg, Förbundet för forskning i socialt arbete

The Doctrine of Saint-Simon: An Exposition 1828-1829 (1958), translated by Iggers, G G, Boston, Beacon Press

Thomas, D (1983) *The Making of Community Work* London, George Allan & Unwin

Towle, C (1954) *The Learner in Education for the Professions* Chicago, University of Chicago Press

von Wright, G H (1986) *Vetenskapen och förnuftet* Stockholm, Bonniers

Wald, L D (1915) *The House on Henry Street* New York, Henry Holt, 1938

Vad är socialt arbete? (1981) Lindholm, K and Askeland, K, Stockholm, Liber

Watts, S J (1984) *A Social History of Western Europe, 1450-1720* London, Hutchinson

Weber, M (1919) *Vetenskap och politik* Göteborg, Korpen, 1977

Weber, M (1949) *The Methodology of the Social Sciences* (eds Shils, E A and Finch, H A) New York, The Free Press

Who's Who in America. *A Biographical Dictionary of Notable Living Men and Women of the United States* (1935), vol 18, Chicago, A N Marquis

Wilsnack, W H (1946) 'Handling resistance in social casework' *American Journal of Orthopsychiatry* 16(1), pp297-311

Wuthnow, R (1991) *Acts of Compassion. Caring for Others and Helping Ourselves* Princeton, University of Princeton Press

Yin, R K (1989) *Case Study Research. Design and Methods* London, Sage Publications

Zeitlin, I M (1968) *Ideology and the Development of Sociological Theory* Englewood Cliffs, Prentice-Hall, 1981

Zimbalist, S E (1977) *Historic Themes and Landmarks in Social Welfare Research* New York, Harper & Row

Index